Competent
Crew

Other titles of interest

Day Skipper
3rd edition
Pat Langley-Price and Philip Ouvry
ISBN 0 7136 6223 9
A clear and simple introduction to pilotage, navigation
and general boatwork for anyone intending to make a
coastal passage. It covers both the theory and the
practical aspects of the RYA Day Skipper Certificate.

Sailing
A Beginner's Guide
David Seidman
ISBN 0 7136 6081 3
This book guides the novice sailor through their first
tentative steps aboard, and then beyond to navigation,
safety and seamanship, conveying the magic as well
as the basic elements of sailing.

Learn to Navigate
4th edition
Basil Mosenthal
ISBN 0 7136 6870 9
With its relaxed, lively style and plentiful illustrations,
this is the simplest, most straight forward introduction
there is. Ideal for novices of all ages.

Knots in Use
3rd edition
Text and photographs by Colin Jarman
Drawings by Bill Beavis
ISBN 0 7136 6710 9
A pocket book of useful and practical knots, bends,
hitches, whippings and splices with drawings showing
how to tie the knots and photos showing how to use
them.

Competent Crew

THIRD EDITION

Pat Langley-Price & Philip Ouvry

ADLARD COLES NAUTICAL
London

Published 2004 by Adlard Coles Nautical
an imprint of A & C Black (Publishers) Ltd
37 Soho Square, London W1D 3QZ
www.adlardcoles.com

First edition published by Adlard Coles 1985
Reprinted 1986, 1987, 1990
Second edition published by Adlard Coles Nautical 1991
Reprinted 1995, 1997
Third edition 2000
Fourth edition 2004

ISBN 0 7136 7089 4

A CIP catalogue record for this book is available from the
British Library.

A & C Black uses paper produced with elemental, chlorine-free pulp,
harvested from managed sustainable forests.

Note: While all reasonable care has been taken in the preparation of
this publication, the author and publisher accept no responsibility for
any errors or omissions or consequences ensuing upon the use of the
methods, information or products described in the book.

Typeset in 11.5pt on 13pt Rotis Semi Serif
Printed and bound in Great Britain by
Cromwell Press, Trowbridge, Wiltshire.

Contents

Acknowledgements

Extracts from the Convention on the International Regulations for Preventing Collision at Sea 1972 are reproduced courtesy of the International Maritime Organisation.

Introduction

Going to sea in a small boat is an activity which many people enjoy; yet to those who have not grown up within sight of the sea, the thought of bobbing about all day in unfamiliar surroundings may not be appealing. However, when the sun is shining, the companionship enjoyable and the fresh air invigorating, the whole idea suddenly seems more attractive and the desire to learn takes hold.

Yet everything is so unfamiliar. There are ropes, shackles and sails, all of which have to be tied together with a variety of knots, bends and hitches; there's coming alongside and casting off, rowing the dinghy and man overboard drill. . . Does this mean that there may be emergencies to deal with? Yes: there are safety regulations, collision rules, fire precautions, weather forecasts and so on to learn about. At sea, safety is paramount and everybody who ventures out on the water must be fully aware of the potential dangers. Feeling safe leads to greater confidence. Greater confidence leads to greater enjoyment. And enjoyment is what cruising and sailing is all about.

This book is designed as an introduction to seafaring for the novice sailor who is totally unfamiliar with boats, sailing and navigating at sea. Everything is explained from first principles, and many diagrams and a glossary at the back are included to help make the nautical language more understandable.

At the same time, not only will the increasingly competent crew want to know what he (or she – we are not being sexist here, merely economical with words) is expected to do, but he will also want to understand what the skipper and navigator are doing. So without going into detail about the theory of navigating or weather forecasting or the International Regulations for Preventing Collisions at Sea, this book includes much of the information that a skipper himself would find useful.

At sea, a boat may be some distance away from other boats and harbours; the weather can get worse, the sea becomes rough and the crew feel tired, cold and seasick. Suddenly a pleasant voyage becomes tinged with apprehension. It is now that a skipper really appreciates a competent crew. And what happens if an accident befalls the skipper? Can he be confident that the crew can cope with getting help and sailing the boat home safely? Could *you* be confident that you could get the boat home? This book sets out to give you just that confidence.

About the book

The contents of this book are based on the syllabus of the Royal Yachting Association's practical course for Competent Crew. All items on this syllabus are covered, together with much additional information of use to beginners as well as more experienced sailors. It must be emphasised that there is no substitute for practical experience, and shorebased and practical learning should go hand-in-hand.

The book has been prepared in two parts:

Part A

This gives the sequence of events that you might encounter on joining a boat going out to sea for the day, either sailing or motoring, and returning that evening to a harbour or to an anchorage. The responsibilities of the skipper and crew are outlined. The skipper is often the navigator, but sometimes the navigator is another member of the crew. Both the skipper and the navigator always appreciate assistance from a keen and competent crew, and will normally be only too willing, in return, to explain why things are done in a certain way.

Part B

This section of the book gives more detail of various aspects of navigation, weather forecasting, collision rules, emergency procedures, and includes information on first aid, fire precautions, engine maintenance, special manoeuvres and sailing etiquette. Finally, there are question and answer papers and a full glossary of nautical terms.

We would like to wish all readers many days of happy and enjoyable sailing and cruising. We are also keen that this book should be complete and unambiguous and would welcome, via the publisher, correspondence that would enable future editions to be improved.

Pat Langley-Price and Philip Ouvry

1 • A New Language

'Belay the main halyard to the cleat on the starboard side of the mast.' A typical request heard on a sailing boat, but incomprehensible to a non-sailing person.

To enjoy sailing or cruising in small boats, you need to feel confident; and feeling safe is the best way to inspire confidence. To feel safe it is important to know what everything on a boat is for, and how to use it; and to understand instructions given by the skipper – the person in charge. Yes, there has to be *one* person in charge. It is difficult to run a boat by committee, so it is better to have one person whose knowledge and experience is respected by everyone else on board and who has the responsibility of making decisions when required.

Every crew member must respect the authority of the skipper, because accidents and emergencies are often caused by lack of discipline on board: not a military discipline but one of basic understanding and respect. To achieve this, crew members must be able to communicate effectively. It is essential that everyone on board understands the terminology and should know how to carry out required actions.

In Appendix III there is a glossary of sea terms which gives a reference source for any unfamiliar words or terms which you come across. Any sailing terms shown in italics in the text will have entries in the glossary.

2 • About the Boat

Types of sailing boat

Sailing boats vary considerably from simple dinghies and day boats with auxiliary engines to motor boats with sails, sailing boats with engines, and motor sailers. A motor sailer has a powerful enough engine to complete a passage under power, but a sufficient spread of sail to make good speed with the wind abeam or abaft without the use of the engine.

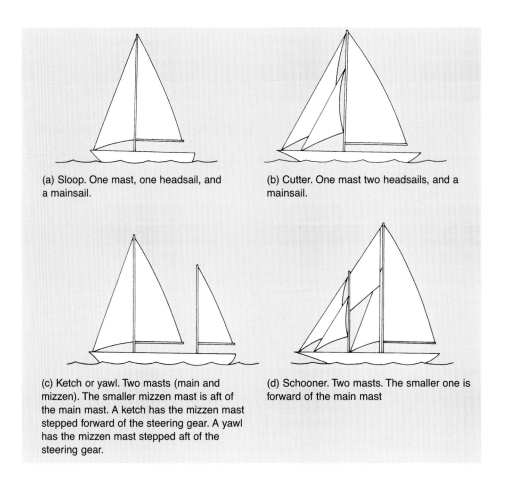

(a) Sloop. One mast, one headsail, and a mainsail.

(b) Cutter. One mast two headsails, and a mainsail.

(c) Ketch or yawl. Two masts (main and mizzen). The smaller mizzen mast is aft of the main mast. A ketch has the mizzen mast stepped forward of the steering gear. A yawl has the mizzen mast stepped aft of the steering gear.

(d) Schooner. Two masts. The smaller one is forward of the main mast

Fig 2.1 Boat rigs.

Rigging

Boats can be rigged in many different ways (Fig. 2.1 shows the most common rigs) but no matter how a boat is rigged, the same general principles of seamanship apply. The most common type of yacht rig (and the standard rig used in this book) is an auxiliary Bermudan sloop – a single-masted sailing boat with a triangular mainsail, a headsail and a low-powered auxiliary engine.

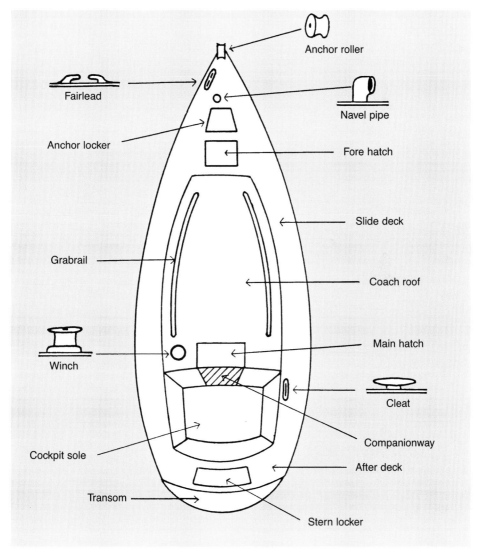

Fig 2.2 Deck plan showing parts of the boat.

Running rigging

This consists of movable lines or wires attached to sails or *spars*, for example, a *halyard* attached to the head of the sail in order to hoist it.

Standing rigging

This term refers to non-movable wires attached between spars and the boat, used for support or tensioning. An example is the *backstay*, which supports the mast and can be tensioned to alter mast bend.

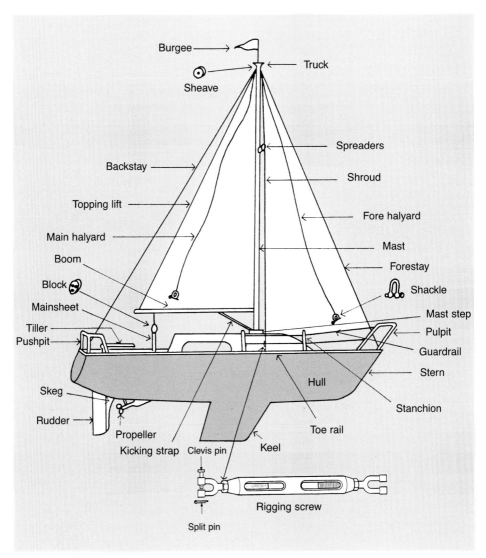

Fig 2.3 Profile plan showing parts of the boat.

Figs 2.2, 2.3, 2.4 and 2.5 all show the various named parts of the boat which you need to know.

Definitions of sailing terms given in italics will be found in the Glossary (Appendix III).

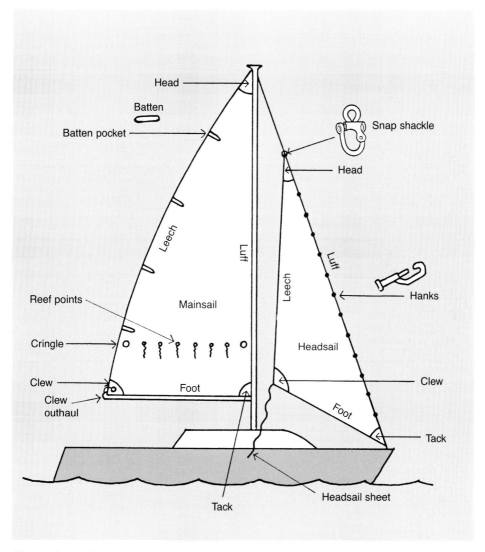

Fig 2.4 Parts of the sail.

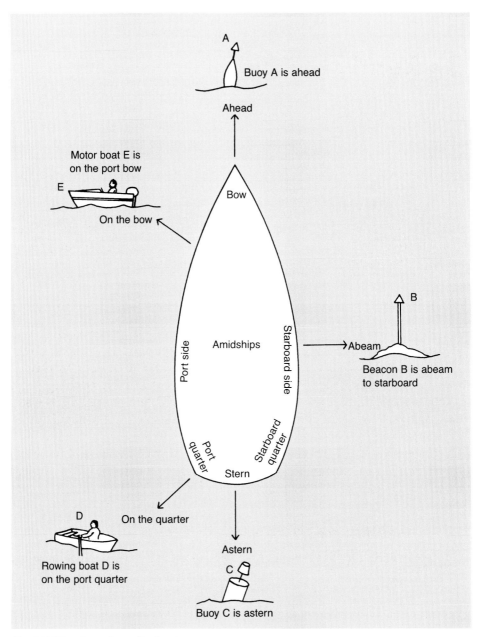

Fig 2.5 Directions from the boat.

3 • Ready to Sail

A 10-metre boat may look fine at a boat show or in a marina, however it will seem very small when six people arrive with all their gear for a week's holiday. There is usually only enough room for sailing clothes and one set of shore clothes, and these will be stored bundled up in a soft bag rather than hanging in a wardrobe.

Everything on board must be stowed in its correct place, normally accessible where it will be required. It is important that everyone knows *exactly* where everything is: from coffee/milk/sugar to the bilge pump; from the hand-bearing compass to the spare torch battery.

What to wear

The wind at sea is extremely chilling, and once you get cold it is very difficult to warm up again. Always have plenty of warm clothes – take double the number you may think you need – and remember to include thick socks, gloves and a woolly hat. On top of the warm clothing, wear waterproof and windproof clothing such as oilskins and anoraks. Shoes and boots should also be waterproof with soft non-slip soles, both for safety and to prevent marking the boat's deck.

Fewer clothes are required in hot weather but do not forget suntan lotion, sunglasses (which can prevent headaches caused by glare) and a sunhat. Remember: the weather can change fast.

Personal safety equipment

In rough weather and at night, everyone on deck should wear a safety harness which should be clipped on to a strong part of the boat such as a fitting bolted through the deck, or a line running the length of the deck which is secured to such fittings. The safety harness line can also be passed around a secure fitting and hooked back on to itself.

When coming up from below in rough weather clip your harness on to a strong fitting in the cockpit before leaving the cabin. Then, before leaving the cockpit to go on deck, transfer it to a suitable deck fitting. When moving along the deck, keep your body low and always hold on to a secure fitting such as the grabrail. It is better to move along the uphill side of the deck so that if you lose your balance, the tendency will be to roll towards the middle of the boat. Never clip on to a guardrail as it may not take the strain if subjected to a sudden jerk, or to standing rigging which can pull out if the boat is dismasted. Sometimes harnesses are incorporated in oilskin jackets, but generally they are separate and are worn outside clothing. Ideally, harnesses should have two clips, so that you are clipped on at all times when moving between different points on the boat. The safety line should prevent you from falling off the boat and so should not be too long. Each crew member should be allocated their own safety harness which should be adjusted to fit ready for immediate use.

Lifejackets should also be allocated to everyone on board. They should be worn:

- If there is a possibility that the boat may have to be abandoned
- In thick fog
- When going ashore in the dinghy
- By all non-swimmers.

Lifejackets are brightly coloured yellow or orange so that they can be seen easily in the water, and often have retro-reflective strips on the collars to aid night-time retrieval from the water. Some are fitted with whistles and small waterproof lights for greater safety.

When buying a lifejacket the important elements to consider are size and buoyancy. A lifejacket should support you on your back when fully clothed, with your head clear of the water. Some lifejackets have to be inflated orally whilst others are self-inflating. The latter are inflated either by squeezing the lever of a carbon dioxide cylinder contained within the lifejacket, or they may inflate automatically on immersion in water.

A buoyancy aid is *not* the same thing as a lifejacket and will only assist the wearer to float. Some types can be further inflated orally so that they become a lifejacket. All safety harnesses and lifejackets must be of a suitably approved type.

Finally, a sharp knife should be included in your personal safety equipment as it may be necessary to cut a rope quickly in an emergency.

Preparing the boat for sea

The following is a typical check list for a boat preparing to set sail. Whilst it is the skipper's responsibility to see these requirements are carried out, much of the routine work on the boat is delegated to the crew, and it is important everyone understands exactly what is required.

- All gear, both above and below deck, properly stowed so that it cannot roll out of place
- Engine checked ready for starting, with all cooling water seacocks open
- Water tanks full
- Fuel tanks full
- Gas bottles and gas taps turned off, spare full gas bottle available
- Crew briefed on emergency procedures including how to launch and board the liferaft; action to take in case of man overboard; when and how to fire flares; *Mayday* procedures
- Crew supplied with seasickness tablets as required
- All electronic instruments and radios checked for operation
- Charts, almanacs and navigational instruments available and up to date
- All safety equipment checked and ready for use
- Navigation lights, torches and flares checked and ready if any night sailing is intended
- Dinghy serviceable, secure and easily accessible
- Lifebuoys, *dan buoys* and safety lines rigged and checked. Crew should be shown the clip-on points to use when wearing a safety harness
- Weather forecast obtained
- *Seacocks* on toilets and sinks in seagoing position
- All hatches secured
- Anchor secure and end of chain or warp made fast inboard
- Bilge pumps checked
- Fire extinguishers accessible and available
- Fire blanket accessible
- Battery switch on
- Remove sail covers if fitted
- *Burgee* and *ensign* hoisted
- All mooring lines ready for slipping

4 • Getting Underway

One of the first jobs you will be required to do once on board is to *bend on* (prepare) the sails. This is best done before the boat leaves her berth, so that the sails can be hoisted as soon as she is all clear.

Bending on the mainsail

Unless the boat has not been used for some time the *mainsail* will already be fitted to the boom. If it is not, starting with the *clew*, feed the *foot* of the sail into the track on the *boom* and pull it along the boom. When it is all fed in, secure the *tack* and tension the foot of the sail by adjusting the *clew outhaul* (Fig 4.1). Now fit the *battens* (stiffeners).

If there are *slides* along the *luff*, feed these into the mast track (starting either with the head or the tack of the sail according to the type of mast track fitting) and push the securing pin into the mast after the last one to stop them

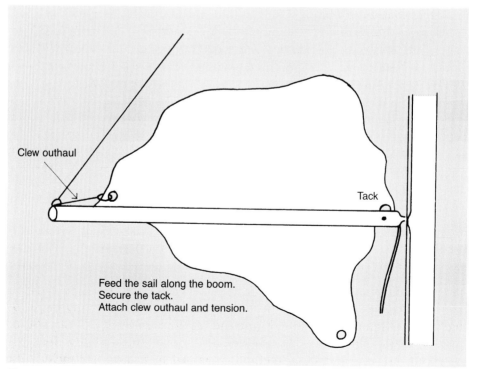

Clew outhaul

Tack

Feed the sail along the boom.
Secure the tack.
Attach clew outhaul and tension.

Fig 4.1 Bending on the mainsail.

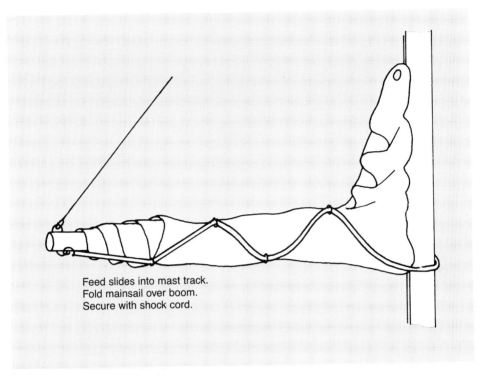

Feed slides into mast track.
Fold mainsail over boom.
Secure with shock cord.

Fig 4.2 Securing the mainsail.

falling out. If the sail has a rope along the luff (bolt rope) instead of slides, do not feed this into the track until the sail is hoisted. It is usually better not to attach the halyard until the sail is about to be hoisted, because without tension on it can get caught up round the *spreaders*, especially in gusty winds. However, if the halyard is fitted without immediately hoisting the sail, a good way to make sure that enough tension is maintained is to temporarily lead the halyard from the head of the sail down around a mast winch or cleat so that the pull on the halyard then pulls the head of the sail downwards whilst the sail remains stowed. Any foul-ups aloft should then be avoided.

Finally, fold the mainsail neatly over the boom and secure it with shock cord (thick elastic) or sail ties (Fig 4.2).

Bending on the headsail

Most cruising boats carry several sizes of *headsail* but the same principle applies whatever the size. The headsail is secured to the *forestay* by *piston hanks* or, in some cases, it fits into a groove on the forestay. It can also be permanently rigged and furled (rolled) around the forestay for easy handling, however the basic method described here does not include the self-furling headsail.

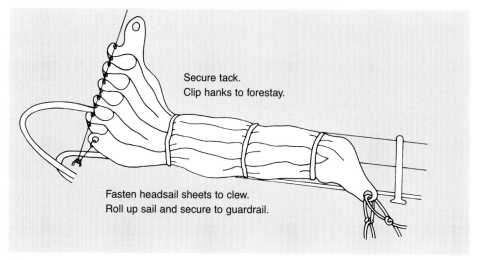

Secure tack.
Clip hanks to forestay.

Fasten headsail sheets to clew.
Roll up sail and secure to guardrail.

Fig 4.3 Bending on and securing the headsail.

Locate the tack (normally the corner bearing the sailmaker's name), and *shackle* it to the appropriate fitting on the *stemhead*. Next, clip the piston hanks to the forestay making sure that they are all the same way round so that the luff of the sail is not twisted. Now run your hand along the foot of the sail from the tack to the clew to check that it is not twisted, then secure the headsail sheets to the clew using bowline knots (or sometimes a shackle) and lead them through the appropriate *blocks* to the *sheet winches*. Tie a *stopper knot* in the ends of the sheets (see Chapter 10). There is no need to fit the halyard to the head of the sail until it is ready to be hoisted; if it *is* fitted; the head of the sail should be secured to the *pulpit* so that tension can be kept on the halyard without the sail being pulled up.

Finally, lay the sail along the deck, roll it up and secure it to the *guardrail* with shock cord or sail ties (Fig 4.3).

Starting the engine

It is sensible to use the engine to get the boat clear of her berth before hoisting the sails. Before starting the engine, put the gear lever into neutral, open the throttle and ensure that the cooling water seacock is open. Most engines are started with an ignition switch and a starter button. As soon as the engine is running, make sure that cooling water is circulating (usually by looking at the cooling water outlet). Diesel engines can be used as soon as they are started and do not like to idle too long. Petrol engines perform better when they have warmed up a little.

To stop a petrol engine, turn off the ignition. A diesel engine usually has a separate stop lever which must be reset before the engine is used again.

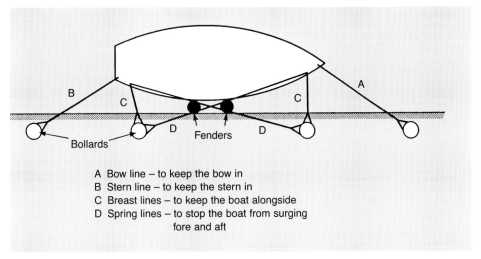

A Bow line – to keep the bow in
B Stern line – to keep the stern in
C Breast lines – to keep the boat alongside
D Spring lines – to stop the boat from surging
        fore and aft

Fig 4.4 Securing with several lines. Fenders protect the boat from damage alongside.

Preparing the mooring lines for leaving the berth

Unless a tidal stream is running, or a strong wind blowing, leaving a berth in a marina or alongside a quay is straightforward. The boat will be secured by several lines as shown in Fig 4.4. All lines except *breast lines* are removed, coiled and stowed. The breast lines are doubled back around a *cleat* or *bollard* on the shore so that they can be let go from on board the boat; these become slip lines (Fig 4.5).

If there is a tidal stream running, leave one line (usually a *spring*) attached until the last moment to stop the boat moving forwards or backwards (depending upon the direction of the tidal stream). This spring can also be doubled back as a slip line. The skipper may detail a crew member to stand by on deck with a spare fender (a *roving fender*) to fend off from any danger.

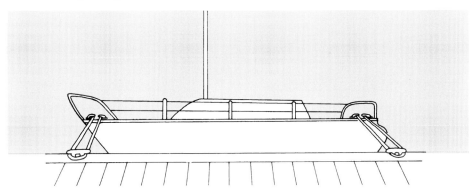

Fig 4.5 Slip lines doubled back around cleats.

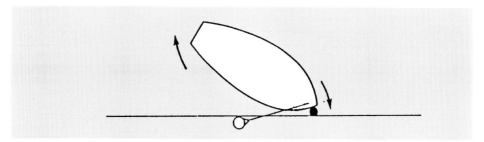

Fig 4.6 Fender positioned between bow and pontoon.

It may be necessary to move the stern of the boat away from the pontoon by motoring forward against a spring line which has been passed around a bollard ashore. One end of the line is secured to the bow *cleat* and the other end held by a crew member by passing a turn around the cleat. A *fender* is placed between the bow of the boat and the pontoon (Fig 4.6).

Leaving a raft of boats

Leaving a mooring is more complicated if your boat is in the middle of a raft of boats moored alongside each other. Often there is no one available to assist on adjacent boats. In this case, you will need to make allowance for the tidal stream if there is any, and cast off (unfasten) sufficient lines to create a gap through which to depart; then manoeuvre the boat slowly (by hauling on lines) until it is clear to leave. Finally, make sure that all the other boats are properly secured. It may be necessary for the skipper to leave a crew member behind to ensure that the other boats are secure, picking him up later from the outside boat of the raft (Fig 4.7). In these circumstances it is essential that the crew understands the function of each line and how to secure it without supervision.

Leaving a buoy

If the boat is moored to a buoy there will only be one bow slip line. This is dealt with in greater detail in Chapter 7.

Stowing lines and fenders

As soon as the boat is clear of her berth all lines must be neatly coiled (see Chapter 10) and stowed and all fenders removed and stowed. Any loose ends of rope left lying around are not only untidy and unseamanlike but can lead to an accident or trail overboard with the possibility of getting wrapped around the propeller.

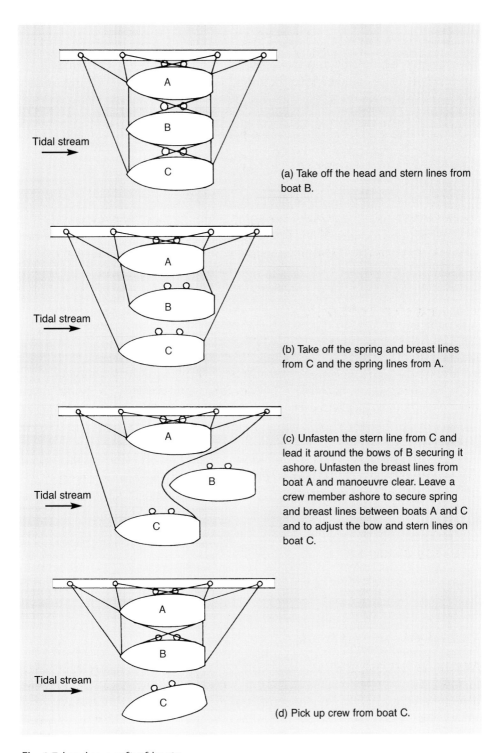

(a) Take off the head and stern lines from boat B.

(b) Take off the spring and breast lines from C and the spring lines from A.

(c) Unfasten the stern line from C and lead it around the bows of B securing it ashore. Unfasten the breast lines from boat A and manoeuvre clear. Leave a crew member ashore to secure spring and breast lines between boats A and C and to adjust the bow and stern lines on boat C.

(d) Pick up crew from boat C.

Fig 4.7 Leaving a raft of boats.

Hoisting the sails

The sails may be hoisted whilst the boat is still in relatively calm waters near the berth. One of the crew may be asked to take the *helm*. Hoisting sails is much easier if the boat is kept moving slowly forward *head to wind*, with all the sheets kept slack so that the wind does not fill the sails. It is also important that everyone keeps a good lookout for other boats and warns the skipper if any appear to be getting too close.

The mainsail

Unshackle the main halyard from its harbour stowage position, check that it is not twisted and shackle it to the head of the mainsail, taking care not to let it go before it is shackled on. The shock cord or sail ties securing the sail can now be released. Turn the boat *head to wind* before hoisting the sail so that the wind does not fill it whilst it is being hoisted. This should prevent the sail from catching on the *spreaders*, but it is always a good idea to keep an eye aloft as the sail goes up to check that nothing gets fouled up.

Release the *kicking strap* and the *mainsheet* so that the boom is free. Lead the halyard around the mainsail winch drum and hoist the sail. (If you are not sure which way the winch drum rotates, spin it by hand first to find out.) It may be necessary to put a couple of extra turns around the winch drum and use the winch handle for the final hoist. Take care not to drop the handle overboard and do not leave it in the winch afterwards. It should be obvious when the sail is completely up; the luff should feel taut but do not over-strain it.

Once the sail is fully hoisted, cleat the halyard, make a coil of the remainder and hang it neatly on the cleat (see Chapter 10). If the halyard is part wire and part rope, all the wire must be turned around the winch drum plus two turns of rope before cleating. Remember that it may be necessary to lower sails in a hurry so *do not* use locking turns that cannot be quickly undone.

Uncleat the *topping lift* and ease it off so that the *leech* of the sail takes the weight of the boom. Tighten the kicking strap, pull in the mainsheet just enough to prevent the boom from swinging from side to side as the sail flaps, and cleat it.

The headsail

The boat does not need to be pointing into wind whilst this sail is being hoisted. Secure the halyard to the head of the sail. Unfasten the shock cord (or sail ties) and check that the sheets are free to run. Turn the halyard around the headsail winch drum and hoist the sail, using the winch handle if necessary. Cleat the halyard and coil the remainder (as for the mainsail).

When the headsail is hoisted and secured, lead the headsail sheet around the sheet winch drum (two turns will be needed initially) and haul it in, using the winch handle if necessary, until it stops flapping. If necessary, put an extra turn around the winch as shown in the photos on page 57, Chapter 10. Be careful not to trap your fingers between the sheet and the winch. When hoisting the headsail keep clear of the flapping sail as this can cause injury, especially if a shackle is fitted to the clew.

When both sails are hoisted the boat can be set on course. Adjust the sheets as necessary once you are underway. It may then be possible to stop the engine.

Do not forget to return any winch handles or sail ties to their proper stowage.

The deck log

As soon as the boat gets underway, the *deck log* (a written record of events), should be entered with the time of departure and relevant details such as: the sails set, engine running hours, wind direction and strength, log reading (from the instrument log which records speed and distance), course, barometric pressure, and so on. This is officially the navigator's responsibility, but every crew member must know how to write up the deck log. Times are shown in four-figure notation using a 24-hour clock, for example 8.00 am is written as 0800 and 8.00 pm is written as 2000. Courses and bearings are given in three-figure notation through 360 degrees.

Lookout

In a small boat the helmsman normally acts as the lookout. However, it is not always easy for him to see around the sails (and other members of the crew), so everyone on deck must be alert at all times to the presence of any approaching boats. Big ships may look a long way off, but they travel at considerable speed and distance can quickly be closed.

5 • Start Sailing

If you have never been on a sailing boat, the mechanics of boat handling seem confusing at first, but a few hours of instruction with an experienced sailor will soon make the essentials clear. If you have sailed a dinghy or sailboard, much of this chapter will be familiar. Keelboats, however, do have their own handling characteristics which must be learnt by sheer practical experience.

The rudder

Unlike a car which is steered by moving the front wheels to the left or right, a boat is steered by the force of the water acting against the rudder at the stern of the boat. As a result the boat's stern is swung to port or starboard, causing the bows to move in the opposite direction (Fig 5.1).

The boat may be steered by using either a tiller or a wheel. A tiller is pushed *away* from the direction in which the bows are to go; a wheel is turned *towards* that direction (Fig 5.2).

Sail trim

The skipper will give instructions to either ease out or haul in the headsail sheet. Look at Fig 5.3 and see whether you can find the relationship between the boat's course and the angle of the sails relative to the wind.

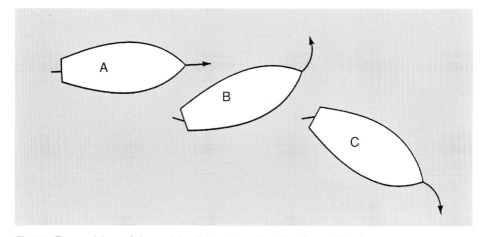

Fig 5.1 The position of the rudder determines the direction of the bow.

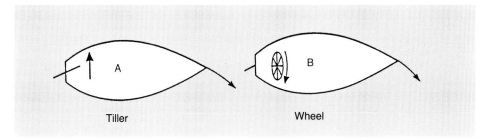

Fig 5.2 Steering by tiller or wheel.

You will see that the further the boat's bows are turned away from the wind, the more the sails are eased out until, when the wind is blowing from behind, the sails are fully out.

Fig 5.4 shows various points of sailing. Knowing exactly how much sail to ease out or take in comes with practical experience, but as a rough guide, *trim* the headsail until it stops flapping, and then adjust the mainsail to the same angle. When the boat is running before the wind, both sails may be on the same side of the boat or one on either side. When the headsail is on the opposite side to the mainsail, the sails are *goosewinged*. Sometimes a spar known as a *whisker pole* is attached to a mast fitting and clipped to the headsail sheet to hold the headsail out. The pole is supported by an

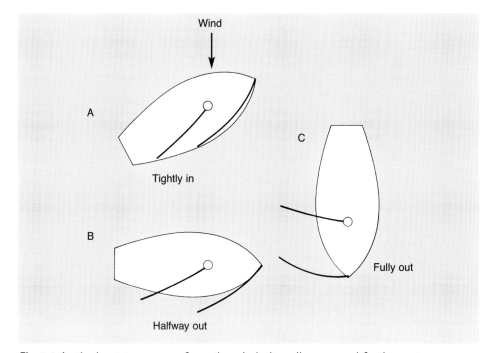

Fig 5.3 As the boat turns away from the wind, the sails are eased further out.

19

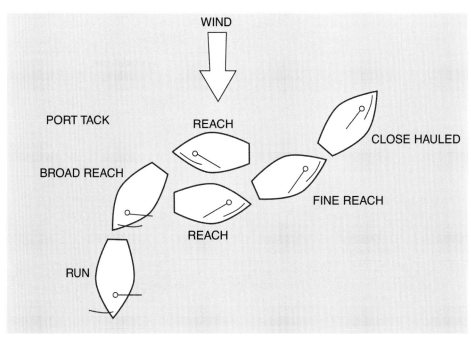

Fig 5.4 Points of Sailing.

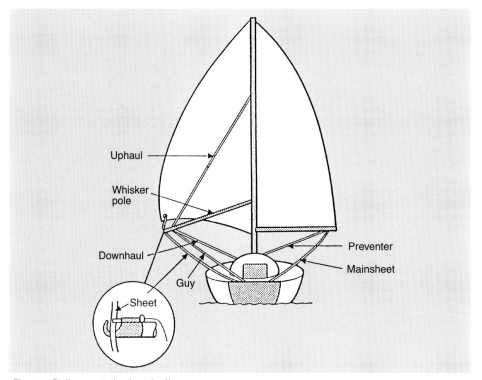

Fig 5.5 Poling out the headsail.

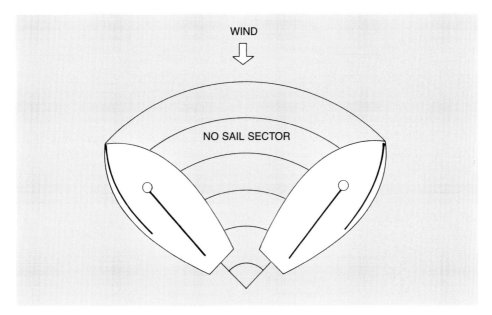

Fig 5.6 The boat cannot sail in the NO SAIL SECTOR.

uphaul, and a *downhaul* stops it rising. There may also be a *guy line* to set the *fore-and-aft* position (Fig 5.5).

No sail sector

No sailing boat can sail directly into the wind. Some sail closer than others but about 45 degrees off the wind is normal on each side, so there will be a *no sail secto*r of about 90 degrees as shown in Fig 5.6.

Sailing upwind

To reach a position directly upwind it is necessary to sail a series of zig-zag courses either side of the wind's direction. This manoeuvre is called *beating* to windward (Fig 5.7). Each course is known as a *tack*.

Naming the tack

In Fig 5.8. Boat A has the wind on the starboard side and the boom is over the port side; she is on *starboard* tack. Boat B has the wind on the port side and the boom over the starboard side; she is on *port* tack. The tack is named *opposite* to the side over which the main boom lies.

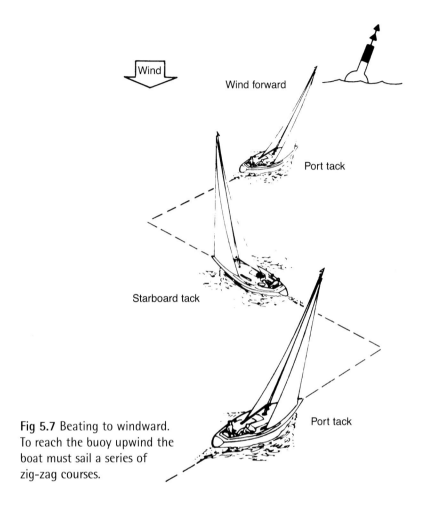

Fig 5.7 Beating to windward. To reach the buoy upwind the boat must sail a series of zig-zag courses.

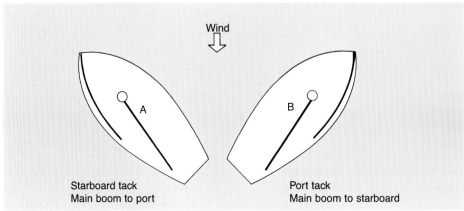

Fig 5.8 Starboard and port tacks.

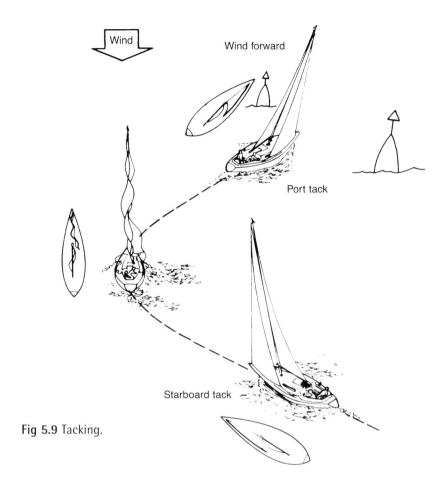

Fig 5.9 Tacking.

Tacking

The action of altering course from one tack to another when the bows of the boat move through the no sail sector is called *going about* or *tacking*. The boat in Fig 5.9 is initially on starboard tack. To go about, the helmsman alerts the crew by saying 'ready about'. When the crew are ready he moves the tiller towards the leeward side of the boat saying 'lee-oh'. This brings the boat's bows towards the wind. A crew member casts off the port headsail sheet and, as the bows move towards and through the wind, the sails flap and then fly across the boat to the other side. The crew now turns the headsail sheet around the starboard winch drum, hauls it in (using a winch handle if necessary) and cleats it. If the mainsail needs adjusting this can be done by the helmsman, but when tacking from close hauled (close to the wind) to close hauled, the mainsheet can normally be left cleated. The boat now sails off on port tack.

Gybing

In Fig 5.10 the boat is initially running on starboard tack with the wind astern. She wishes to pass around the buoy ahead and then alter course to port. To do this she has to perform a manoeuvre known as a *gybe*, in which the stern of the boat passes through the eye of the wind.

As the buoy is approached, the helmsman alerts the crew by saying 'stand by to gybe'. When the crew are ready he centres the mainsheet traveller, hauls in the mainsheet fully and cleats it. This stops the boom flying dangerously from one side of the boat to the other. He then moves the tiller to starboard, making the boat's stern travel through the wind, and warns the crew that the boom is about to come across the boat by saying 'gybe-oh'. As the boom crosses the boat and the wind fills the sail on the other side, he centres the tiller and eases out the mainsheet again. At the same time, the crew eases out the port headsail sheet and hauls in the starboard one, taking care not to let the headsail fly forward as it may get twisted around the forestay. The boat is now running on port tack, ready to alter course to round the buoy. The boat's course should remain fairly steady as the boat gybes.

Preventer

To help prevent an accidental gybe, you can rig a line called a *preventer*. This is attached to the end of the main boom, led forward outside all rigging, and passed through the bow fairlead back aft to the cockpit (Fig 5.5). In congested areas, when the skipper may be repeatedly altering course, a preventer is not fitted and the headsail is not poled out.

Steering a course

When close hauled the course steered is dictated by the wind direction. The helmsman endeavours to keep the boat sailing with the sails full (not flapping), allowing for any slight shifts in wind direction. He assesses the mean direction he can steer and tells the navigator.

When reaching or running the helmsman will be given a course to steer by the navigator. Usually the navigator will give the helmsman a compass course, which will mean using the steering compass. This is explained in Chapter 12.

As a crew member, you will be expected to take your turn at the helm. You may find it tricky at first to sail close hauled because if the wind gets behind the sails the boat will accidentally tack. Similarly when running, the wind can get behind the mainsail and cause a gybe. Constant practice with an experienced skipper is the only way to learn.

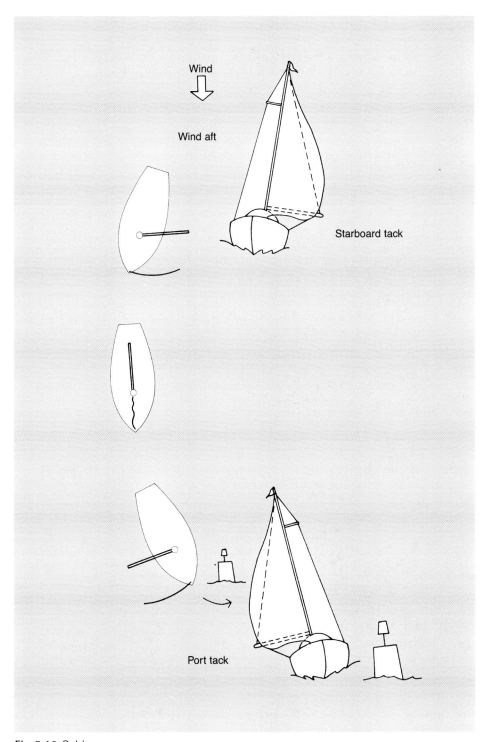

Wind

Wind aft

Starboard tack

Port tack

Fig 5.10 Gybing.

6 ● Coming into Harbour

You will find it very satisfying when you enter a harbour, particularly a strange one, and secure to a berth smartly, efficiently and quietly. The procedure for entering harbour must be worked out in advance. If the engine is to be used it must be started and the sails lowered in the approaches to the harbour.

Approach

When entering an unfamiliar harbour, the navigator will require the crew's assistance in sighting landmarks, taking bearings, watching the depth and identifying leading marks or lights.

Bear in mind the possibility of engine failure or the propeller being fouled, and make ready both the anchor and a fender.

If there is no alongside berth available, it may be necessary to pick up a buoy or moor to piles, and so the dinghy should be made ready.

Lowering the sails

The skipper will decide which sail to lower first. This will depend on many factors, but having the boat under optimum control will be his aim as he approaches harbour.

The mainsail
The boat should be pointed into the wind to make lowering the mainsail easier and to keep it clear of the spreaders.

Uncleat the mainsheet and kicking strap and tension the topping lift so that it takes the weight of the boom. Uncleat the main halyard and lower the sail. Unfasten the halyard from the head of the sail and secure it in its harbour stowage. Take up any slack and cleat the other end of the halyard. Coil the remainder and hang the

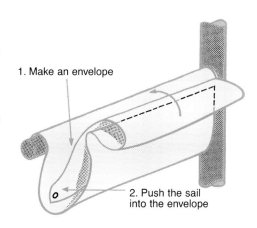

1. Make an envelope

2. Push the sail into the envelope

Fig 6.1 Stowing the mainsail.

coil on the cleat. Haul in and cleat the mainsheet then tighten the kicking strap.

Depending on the time available and the weather conditions, either fold the sail neatly away as shown in Fig 4.2 (Chapter 4) or stow it at the luff and the leech about a metre from the foot, and double it to form an envelope. Push the rest of the sail into this envelope and then tightly roll and secure it. The luff of the sail can either be left in the mast track, or removed as shown in Fig 6.1.

The headsail

The headsail can be lowered without the boat being head to wind. However, if it is flying out over the water, it is easier if one of the crew controls the halyard, letting the sail down slowly to prevent it falling into the water, whilst another crew member in the bows gathers it in.

When the sail is down, take the halyard off the head of the sail and secure it, then take up the slack and cleat it. Coil the remainder and hang it on the cleat. Then either fasten the sail to the guardrail with shock cord or put it into its bag and stow it.

Preparing for berthing

Mooring lines should be secured to the deck cleats fore and aft and led through the *fairleads* ready for use (on both sides if necessary). It is a good idea to secure the outboard ends temporarily to the shrouds, so they are immediately available in the correct position for stepping off the boat, without the possibility of them falling overboard and trailing in the water. The fenders should be rigged in their usual place. As the berth is approached two crew members should be ready to step off the boat with the fore and aft mooring lines.

If sufficient crew are available, the skipper will probably ask one person to stand by with a roving fender, in case the placing of the rigged fenders is not quite right or they are pushed out of position. *It is dangerous to fend the boat off using feet or hands as this can cause serious injury.*

Berthing

The approach is made into the tidal stream, allowing for any wind.

Pontoon berth

As the boat approaches the berth, the two crew members should be ready to step on to the pontoon with the bow and stern lines, taking care not to obstruct the skipper's view. (They should wait until the boat is alongside rather than trying to jump a gap.) Once ashore, the lines should be turned

The crew have made sure that the boat was well fendered before securing bow and stern lines around cleats on the pontoon. Photo: John Goode.

around a cleat or bollard to take the strain and then temporarily secured until permanent lines are rigged. The bows of the boat must not be pulled in too far – just enough to stop the boat alongside.

Quayside berth

The general principles are the same as for pontoon berthing. The top of the quay may be above deck level, however, and so the skipper will come alongside a ladder on the wall. If there are *piles* sticking out from the quay it will be necessary to tie a plank of wood horizontally along the fenders to protect the boat (Fig 6.2). When alongside, the boat is held against the piles whilst crew members climb the ladder with the bow and stern mooring lines and secure these to bollards well forward and aft of the boat's position. Spring and breast lines are then rigged. If there is a tidal rise and fall, the lines must be adjusted regularly.

Quayside berth alongside other boats

As soon as the boat is alongside the outer boat the crew step off and temporarily make the bow and stern lines fast to the fore and aft cleats on the other boat. The crew then rig spring and breast lines to the other boat, taking care that these are led through fairleads where possible so that they do not cause *chafe*. It is important to berth the boat in such a way that the spreaders on the two boats will not hit each other if there is any swell. Bow and stern lines to the shore will also be needed so that inside boats are able

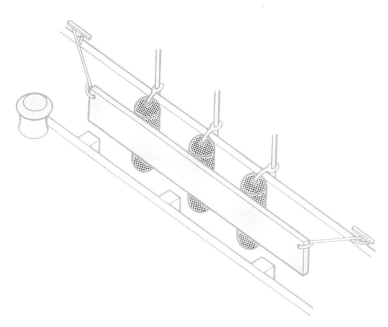

Fig 6.2 A plank used with fenders to protect the boat from quayside piles.

to slip out (Fig 6.3). When several boats are moored to the same bollard, a bow line is passed through the other lines so as not to foul them (Fig 6.4). The rope is taken around the back of the bollard or cleat and then several figure of eight turns are added. Finally the rope may be twisted to form a locking turn but this should not be used on a rope under tension which may need to be released quickly (Fig 6.5).

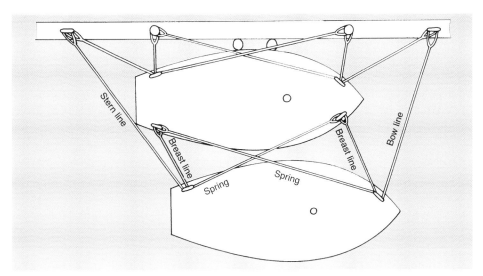

Fig 6.3 Berthing alongside another boat.

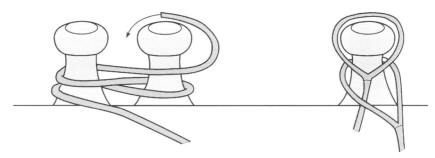

Fig 6.4 and 6.5 Left: When securing to a double bollard or cleat, the warp is turned as a figure of eight between the two posts. The last turn can be a locking turn for security but it is not necessary if enough turns are made. Right: When mooring to a bollard where other boats are already moored, pass lines *under* the existing one before passing them over the bollard.

Berthing between piles or buoys

The approach is made into the tidal stream. If there is already a boat moored between the piles or buoys, the boat comes alongside it. The crew steps onto the moored boat, temporarily making the bow and stern lines fast. They then rig spring and breast lines and the dinghy is used to rig bow and stern lines to the piles or buoys.

If there are no other boats on the mooring, the approach is made to the *upstream* pile or buoy and the bow line is secured. The boat then drops back to the *downstream* pile or buoy and secures the stern line. The bow line is taken in until the boat lies in the centre of the mooring space (Fig 6.6). If there is a cross wind it may be necessary to pick up the bow mooring and use the dinghy to row the stern line aft.

Mooring buoys usually have a large ring to which the line is secured. To avoid chafe, a complete turn is taken around the ring and a long bow line tied. (See also Picking up a mooring Chapter 7, p 39.)

Securing to a pile is a little more difficult. The pile consists of a post which has a vertical metal bar. There is a movable mooring ring around this bar to which a line is attached, so that the ring can be pulled up at any state of the tide (Fig 6.7). The boat is

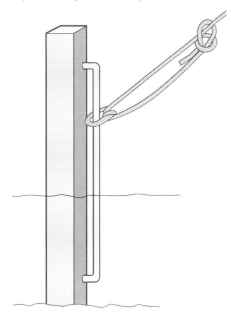

Fig 6.7 Securing to a pile with a movable ring.

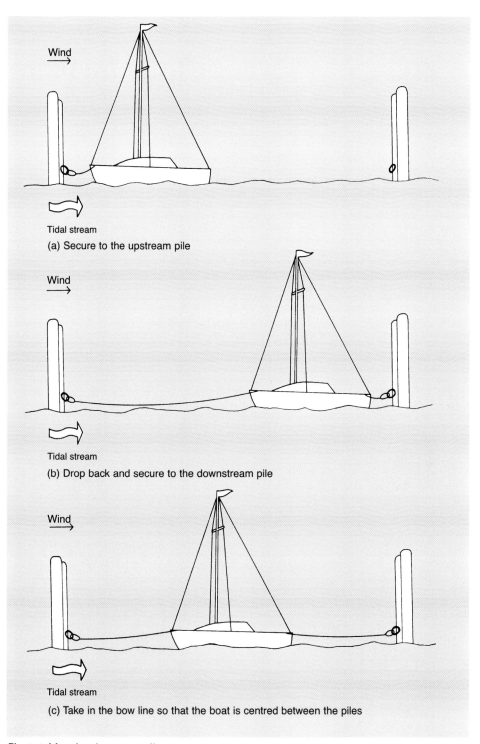

Wind →

Tidal stream
(a) Secure to the upstream pile

Wind →

Tidal stream
(b) Drop back and secure to the downstream pile

Wind →

Tidal stream
(c) Take in the bow line so that the boat is centred between the piles

Fig 6.6 Mooring between piles.

brought alongside the pile and whilst one crew member holds it in position, using a fender if necessary, another of the crew pulls up the ring and passes a line through it. The line should be turned around the ring and a long bow-line tied in it.

After securing

When the boat has been securely berthed or moored, all spare lines and sheets are coiled and stowed. The mainsail should be properly folded (if this has not already been done) and the cover put on. If the boat is not to be used for some time the mainsail can be taken off and stowed. The headsail is folded so that it can be put into its bag and stowed (Fig 6.8).

Finally, make sure the following tasks are completed:

- The boat is cleaned and left shipshape
- All seacocks are put into their harbour position
- Ensign and burgee are left hoisted or lowered as appropriate (see Chapter 15)
- The deck log is completed
- Stocks of fuel, gas and water are checked and replenished if necessary
- A list of defects is made, for attention before the next sail.

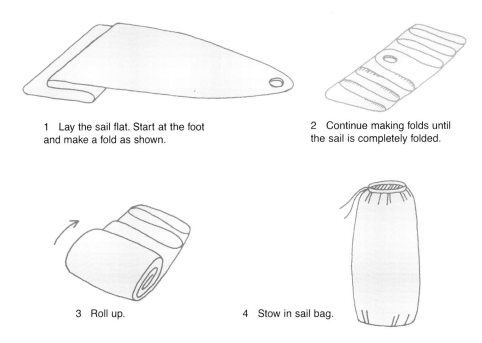

1 Lay the sail flat. Start at the foot and make a fold as shown.

2 Continue making folds until the sail is completely folded.

3 Roll up.

4 Stow in sail bag.

Fig 6.8 Folding a headsail.

7 · Stopping for a While

Choosing an anchorage

When selecting an anchorage your skipper will take the following factors into consideration:

- Is there good holding ground free from obstructions?
- Does it provide maximum shelter from all expected winds?
- Is the area clear of obstructions for when the boat swings?
- Is there sufficient depth of water to avoid going aground?
- Is it away from busy areas frequently used by other boats?
- If it is intended to go ashore, is there a suitable landing place?

The ideal anchorage is one where there are no other boats. A crowded area can lead to awkward situations should the wind shift. Many approaches to pleasant anchorages are not easy and the navigator will need the crew's assistance to find landmarks, take *bearings* and check the depth.

Approaching the anchorage

The approach to an anchorage or a mooring may be made under power or sail. It is important to assess the strength of the tidal stream and its direction in relation to the wind, because this will dictate the line of approach; observing mooring buoys or lobster pots in the immediate vicinity can help with this. The way the boat will finally lie once anchored or moored can best be gauged by looking at other similar boats already there.

Ideally, you should lower the headsail and secure it to the guardrail, to leave the foredeck clear. When the wind and tidal stream are in the same direction, the boat will approach on a fine reach, letting the mainsail fly at the last moment. However, if the wind is against the tidal stream and the tidal stream is stronger than, or the same as the wind, the boat may have to approach on a run. If the mainsail is left up the boat will not be able to stop, so the helmsman should round up into wind before the anchorage or mooring is reached so that the sail can be lowered and secured. The approach will then be made using the headsail only. If you are working on the foredeck with a flapping headsail, take care not to get caught up in the headsail sheets, especially if using a safety harness.

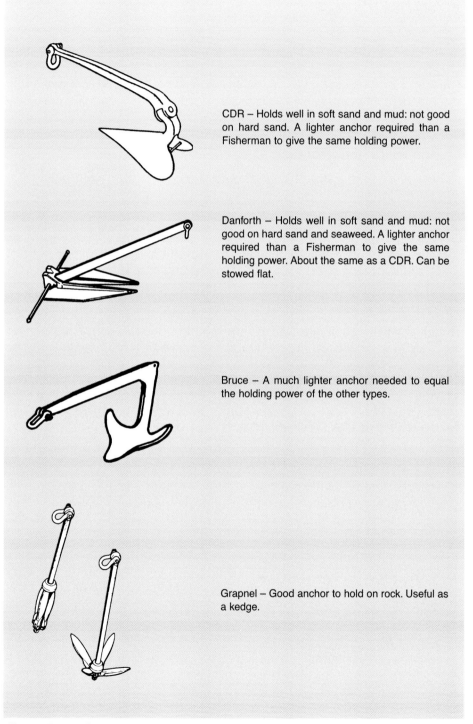

CDR – Holds well in soft sand and mud: not good on hard sand. A lighter anchor required than a Fisherman to give the same holding power.

Danforth – Holds well in soft sand and mud: not good on hard sand and seaweed. A lighter anchor required than a Fisherman to give the same holding power. About the same as a CDR. Can be stowed flat.

Bruce – A much lighter anchor needed to equal the holding power of the other types.

Grapnel – Good anchor to hold on rock. Useful as a kedge.

Fig 7.1 Types of anchor.

Preparing the anchor

Before reaching the anchorage, feed the required length of chain or warp (cable) out of the anchor locker and lay it out on the deck (*flaking*). This ensures that the amount required is immediately ready and that it will not snarl up. Care must be taken to avoid damage to the deck or injury to the crew, particularly if the anchor should go overboard accidentally. If the cable is marked at 5-metre intervals, and it will run freely out of the anchor locker, it need not be flaked.

The amount of anchor cable to be let out (veered) is:

- Four times the maximum expected depth if all chain is used
- Six times the depth if a combination of warp and chain is used
- At least eight times the depth if bad weather is expected

The pull on the anchor exerted by the cable must be horizontal along the seabed if the anchor is to hold securely. This is why all anchor cables should include at least 6 metres of chain attached to the anchor.

The anchor should be held over the anchor roller ready to let go and not dangled over the bows (particularly if there is any swell). Fig 7.1 shows different types of anchor. Fig 7.3 shows the various parts of an anchor.

Letting go the anchor

The crew should wait until the skipper gives the signal to lower the anchor; this will be when the boat has stopped moving forwards over the ground. The skipper will judge this by selecting suitable shore transits. He will also decide exactly *where* to drop the anchor, in relation to: other boats, the depth, the shelter or lack of it from any direction – even how far it is to row ashore. Once the order is given, the anchor is lifted clear of the anchor roller and then lowered (letting the cable roll over the anchor roller) until it reaches the seabed. As the boat drifts backwards, more cable is veered until the predetermined length of cable has been paid out.

The inboard end of the anchor cable is secured to a strong cleat or to the *samson post* so that the rest of the cable will not be pulled out of the anchor locker (Fig 7.2).

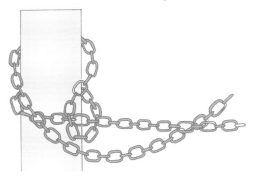

Fig 7.2 Securing the anchor cable to a samson post. The cable is turned around the post. A bight of cable is passed under the standing part and then looped back over the top of the post.

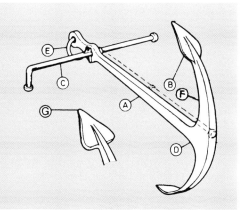

Fig 7.3 Fisherman anchor. This anchor has good holding power in sand and mud and it can be stowed flat. The parts of the Fisherman anchor are as follows: A shank, B fluke, C stock, D crown, E ring, F arm, G bill.

The sails, if still hoisted, are lowered, rolled up and secured.

A black ball should be hoisted in the fore part of the boat to indicate to other boats that you are at anchor. At night an all-round white light should be shown.

Anchor bearings

Because anchors do not always take a firm hold immediately, the navigator should select suitable shore transits or use bearings to check whether the anchor is dragging. He may ask you to check these frequently for him. He should also check the water depth periodically and watch that the boat does not swing into other boats as the tidal stream changes direction or the wind shifts.

Leaving the anchorage

Whether this is done under sail or under power will depend upon the number of boats in the anchorage, the weather conditions and the experience of the crew.

If it is decided to sail off the anchorage and the wind and tidal stream are in the same direction, both sails can be hoisted (although it is preferable to hoist only the mainsail so as to keep the foredeck clear). If the wind and tidal stream are opposite to each other and the boat is lying to the tidal stream, only the headsail should be hoisted at first.

When the helmsman is ready, if the wind is light and the tidal stream weak, the crew should take up the slack anchor cable and feed it into the anchor locker until the boat's bows are directly over the anchor. At this point they should tell the helmsman that the anchor cable is *up and down*. If a *trip line* is attached to a buoy, this should be picked up and any slack line taken in. The anchor should then be *broken out* – extracted from the mud, sand

Fouled anchor

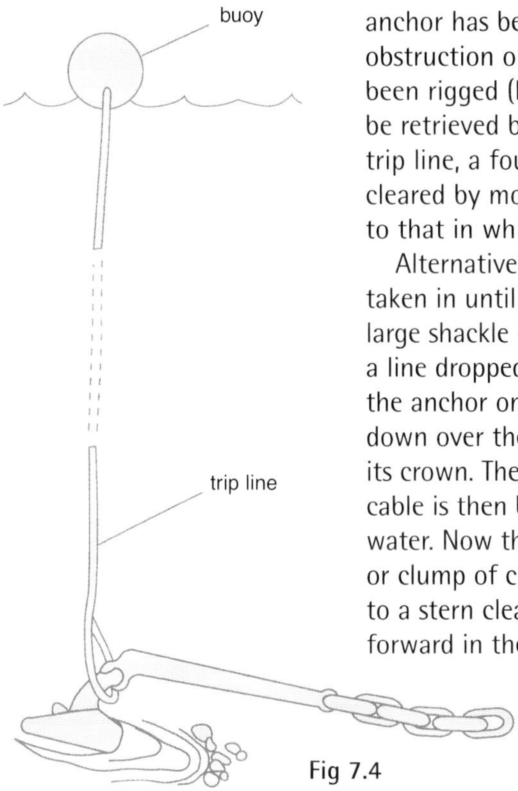

buoy

trip line

Fig 7.4

It can be most aggravating to find that the anchor has become caught fast upon an obstruction on the seabed. If a trip line has been rigged (Fig 7.4) the anchor can usually be retrieved by hauling on this. Without a trip line, a fouled anchor can sometimes be cleared by motoring in the direction opposite to that in which it was laid.

Alternatively, the anchor cable can be taken in until it is up and down, and a really large shackle or a clump of chain secured to a line dropped down around the taut cable to the anchor on the seabed. It should then slip down over the shank of the anchor towards its crown. The inboard end of the anchor cable is then buoyed and dropped into the water. Now the line attached to the shackle or clump of chain on the seabed is made fast to a stern cleat and the boat motored forward in the opposite direction to that in which the anchor was laid. With luck, the slightly lower point of purchase on the anchor will drag it free of the obstruction.

Occasionally an anchor may become so fouled on the seabed that it has to be abandoned. If this happens, it should be buoyed and its position noted so that it can be retrieved later by a diver.

or weed into which it has dug – using the trip line if necessary. The helmsman should also be told when the anchor is off the bottom, and when it is clear of the water. The anchor is then brought on board and secured. If conditions permit it should be scrubbed clean before stowing.

When there is a strong wind or a strong tidal stream, the boat will either have to be sailed or motored up to the anchor's position, with the crew taking in the slack cable as before. In this case they must indicate to the helmsman the direction in which the cable lies from the boat so that he can manoeuvre the boat to take the tension out of the cable.

Kedge anchor

A kedge anchor can be any lightweight anchor with a short length of chain and a warp. It is used for holding a boat in position if the wind drops and there is a foul tide (for example, when racing) or to help pull off a boat that has gone aground. It can also be used in conjunction with the main anchor to prevent yawing in strong winds (Fig 7.5). Figure 7.6 shows how to lay two anchors in order to limit the boat's swinging circle.

Mooring

When approaching a mooring, the procedures are generally the same as for an approach to an anchorage (see Chapter 7).

Picking up a mooring

• *A buoy with a ring*
One member of the crew should be ready in the bows with a boathook. There should be a line made fast at one end to a foredeck cleat. This can be held by a second crew member if one is available. As the boat approaches the buoy, the crew member holding the hook should indicatethe buoy's position to the helmsman.

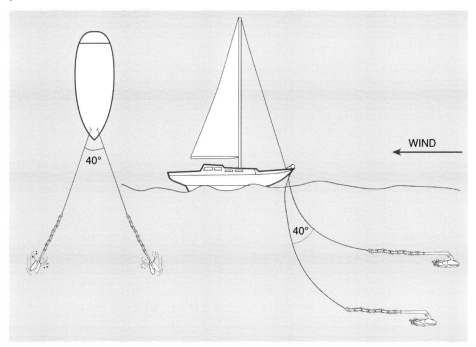

Fig 7.5 Mooring with two anchors to prevent yawing.

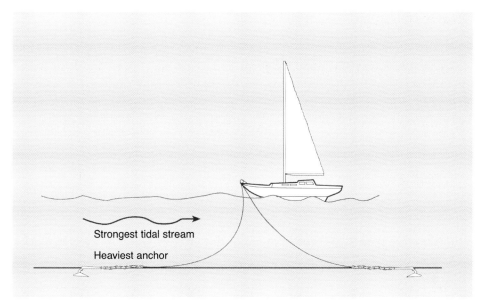

Strongest tidal stream

Heaviest anchor

Fig 7.6 Mooring with two anchors to limit the boat's swinging circle.

When the boat's bows stop alongside the buoy the boathook is used to snag the ring on top of it. (It may be necessary to lie down and reach under the guardrail to achieve this, and the crew member doing this must be clipped on.) The free end of the line is then immediately passed through the ring, brought back on board and cleated. This takes the strain off the boat hook, which can now be retrieved, and holds the boat until a decision can be made as to how to secure more permanently.

When the permanent line is secured, make a round turn around the ring on the buoy and use lengths of hosepipe or rag to protect it from chafe where it passes over the anchor roller or through the fairlead. It is also a good idea to rig a second line, which is left slack, in case the original one fails.

● *A pick-up buoy*
There may be a small buoy floating near to the larger mooring buoy, attached to it by a thin line. This is a pick-up buoy. Approach the mooring in the same way as before, but bring the boat's bow alongside the pick-up buoy. Again, use the boathook to snag the line under the pick-up buoy, which is brought back on board. Connect the line on the buoy to a heavy warp or chain in which there is an eye. Haul the mooring buoy warp or chain on board, passing it over the anchor roller and make fast to a cleat or samson post. It is not a good idea to use the thin line on the pick-up buoy for securing, as this may not take the strain.

Leaving a mooring

If the wind and tidal stream are in the same direction, both sails or just the mainsail can be hoisted. If the wind is against the tidal stream, only the headsail will be used initially, with the boat rounding up into wind to hoist the mainsail when clear. The crew should rig a slip line or uncleat the mooring chain and hold it on one turn around the cleat ready to let go. If the headsail is hoisted this can be backed to ensure that the boat's bows pay off in the desired direction.

In crowded moorings the skipper may decide to do these manoeuvres under power.

Using the dinghy

A dinghy or boat's tender is used to get ashore from an anchorage or mooring. There are many different types of dinghy – inflatables are widely used – but the rules are the same for each:

- It is advisable to wear lifejackets as accidents can happen, especially at night
- Make sure the dinghy is securely fastened to the boat by its painter before launching
- If it is necessary to fit an outboard motor, fasten a line to this before lowering it into the dinghy and, when in position, secure it so that if it jumps off the bracket it will not be lost
- Be careful to avoid fuel spillage
- Do not allow the painter to hang in the water as it can foul the propeller
- Always carry oars in case of engine failure
- Carry a torch to indicate your position to other boats at night.

A dinghy is usually boarded via a ladder alongside or at the stern of the boat. Never jump into a dinghy; it may capsize or the floor can be damaged. The oarsman should get in first and the oars are then handed aboard. The rest of the crew can then board one at a time, stepping carefully into the middle of the dinghy, distributing the weight evenly. It may be necessary to fit an extension tiller for the outboard motor for better balance. Never stand up or make sudden movements as this can cause a capsize.

If there is a strong wind or tidal stream it will be necessary to compensate by pointing the bows of the dinghy towards it (Fig 7.7). An inflatable dinghy is difficult to manoeuvre both under oars and power, and if you are not used to boat handling, practice in calm conditions is advisable.

If the dinghy is moored ashore, it may be necessary to leave a long painter to allow for the fall of the tide. Oars left in the dinghy must be well secured.

If approaching a beach, stop the engine and tilt it to avoid damage to the propeller. If necessary, be ready to get out and prevent the dinghy from running on to rocks or shingle. It can then be carried up the beach to a safe position.

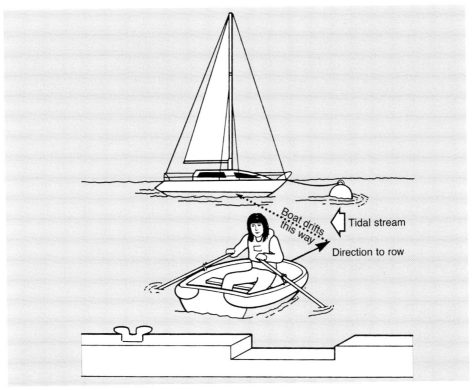

Fig 7.7 Allowing for the tidal stream.

When launching from a beach, walk the dinghy to rowing depth and get in. If using the outboard motor, row into sufficient depth before lowering then starting it. Do not stand in the water by the dinghy when starting the motor.

On your return to the boat, an inflatable dinghy can be deflated, stowed on board and lashed down or secured alongside as shown in Fig 7.8. Rowlocks should be removed. Except in calm weather it is not a good idea to tow a dinghy behind the boat as it can easily capsize.

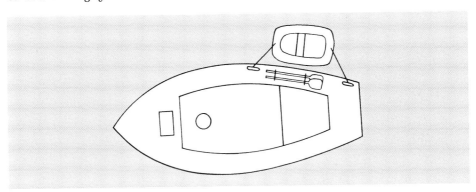

Fig 7.8 Securing the dinghy alongside.

Emergency use of the dinghy

If the boat's engine fails, the dinghy, with outboard engine, can be secured alongside as shown in Fig 7.9 to give the boat some steerage way. This is more effective than towing a heavy keelboat with a light dinghy.

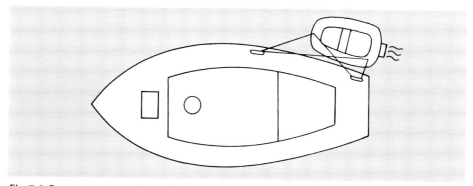

Fig 7.9 Emergency propulsion. For emergency propulsion, springs are needed as well as bow and stern lines.

8 • Bad Weather

The skipper will listen regularly to weather reports and forecasts and so will usually have some prior warning of bad weather (see Chapter 11).

Fog

At the approach of a fog bank or in decreasing visibility, the navigator will immediately try to fix the boat's position using any available landmarks. There will also be a record of fixes in the deck log, so he should know the approximate position of the boat at all times.

There are two major dangers in dense fog:

1 Being run down by a larger boat.

2 Going aground.

Safety in Fog

- Be as quiet as possible, keep a good lookout, and listen for fog signals and other boats' engines. To do this effectively it may be necessary to position a crew member in the bows of the boat, well away from the noise of the boat's own engine
- Wear a lifejacket
- Hoist the radar reflector and make use of any electronic instruments such as the echo sounder and the Global Positioning System (GPS)
- Sound the correct fog signal (see Chapter 14)
- In order to minimise navigational error as much as possible, maintain a steady course and speed. If there is little wind the engine may have to be used, in which case it is a good idea to shut it off periodically to listen out for any approaching boats or fog signals. The skipper will need to decide whether to stay out in deep water or go inshore and anchor.

Gales

If gales are expected the skipper will reduce the area of the mainsail by *reefing,* and set a small headsail, possibly a *storm jib.*

All gear above deck should be securely lashed down and all gear below deck properly stowed and lashed down if necessary. Check all hatches to see that they are secure and the washboards are in position. The cook of the day should prepare sandwiches and hot drinks in vacuum flasks in case it is not practical to do so later.

Seasickness tablets may be needed.

Reefing

The decision to reef is often made too late or the sail area reduced insufficiently. The boat may appear to be sailing well downwind, but she could be greatly overcanvassed if she has to turn into wind in an emergency. Fig 8.1 shows three methods of reefing the mainsail.

Reefing at sea is made easier by *heaving-to* (Fig 8.2). When hove-to, a boat will be steady with little forward movement; she will, however, drift sideways, so plenty of sea-room downwind is required. If it becomes necessary to reef, all crew members on deck must wear a safety harness and be clipped on.

Shaking out a reef

To shake out a reef, the boat may heave-to or continue sailing to windward. Ease out the mainsheet, untie the reefing pennants and lines, and feed the luff of the sail into the mast track. The sail can then be hoisted in the usual manner. It is much easier to shake out a reef than to put one in as the wind is lighter.

Changing a headsail

In calm weather the new headsail can be carried on to the foredeck in the sail bag, which should be secured so that it will not be lost overboard. For the inexperienced sailor, the next step is to lower the existing headsail and either stow it in its bag or secure it along the deck with shock cord. The new headsail is then bent on and hoisted, as explained in Chapter 4. Those with more experience can shackle the new sail on to the forestay below the bottom hank before the existing sail is lowered.

In rough weather do not carry the sail on to the foredeck. Make sure that you are safely clipped on then lower the sail. Unhank it from the head and pass the head along the deck to a crew member waiting in the cockpit. Do not unshackle the tack of the sail until the crew member has the head. Pass the sail below. The tack of the new sail is passed to the crew on the foredeck and shackled on. When this is done, the rest of the sail is fed along the deck. If this procedure is followed, sails will not get lost overboard.

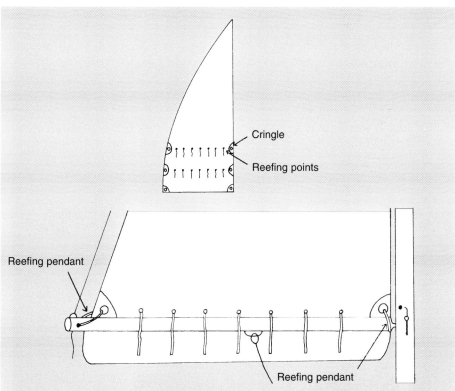

(1) Reefing points. (a) Ease the kicking strap and tension the topping lift. Take the securing pin out of the mast so that the luff of the sail can be pulled out of the mast track. Uncleat the main halyard and lower the mainsail to a position where the luff cringle can be lashed to the boom. (b) Feed a short length of line (called a reefing pendant) through the luff cringle and lash it to the boom. The pendant for the leech cringle may be pemanently attached to one side of the boom and all that is necessary is to pass it through the cringle and secure it to a block on the other side of the boom.

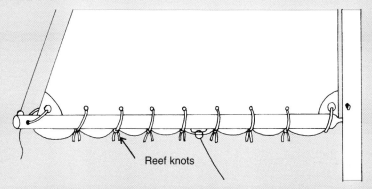

(c) Hoist the sail, replace the securing pin in the mast, cleat the halyard, ease out the toppng lift and tension the kicking strap. (d) Roll up the loose sail and secure by tying together (under the boom) the reefing points from either side of the sail. Use reef knots for this. (e) When taking the reef out, untie the reefing points before the reefing pendants or the sail may tear.

Fig 8.1 Reefing.

Fig 8.1 Reefing continued

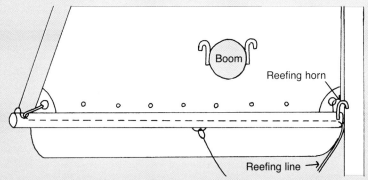

(2) Slab reefing. (a) Ease the kicking strap and tension the topping lift. Take the securing pin out of the mast so that the luff of the sail can be pulled out of the mast track. Uncleat the main halyard and lower the mainsail to a position where the luff cringle can be hooked over the reefing horn. (b) Hook the luff cringle over the reefing horn and pull the leech cringle down to the boom by using the reefing line. (This is attached to the boom near the end, fed through the leech cringle and then back trhough the boom, via a block.)

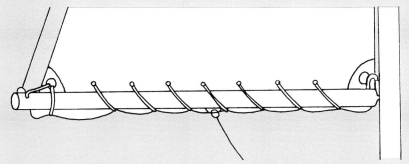

(c) Hoist the sail, replace the securing pin, cleat the halyard, ease out the topping lift and tension the kicking strap. (d) Roll up the loose sail and spiral a light line through the eyelets in the sail and around the boom, securing it at both ends. (e) When taking the reef out, remove the light line first.

(3) Roller reefing.
(a) Take off the kicking strap and tension the topping lift. Take the securing pin out of the mast so that the luff of the sail can be pulled out of the mast track. (b) Uncleat the halyard and ease down the sail, turning the reefing handle at the same time. The sail should pulled tight at the leech to make it roll evenly. Care should be taken to prevent the luff fouling the reefing gear. (c) When the sail has been reduced sufficiently, remove or secure the reefing handle, hoist the sail, replace the securing pin, cleat the halyard and ease out the topping lift. With this method any amount of sail can be reduced, but the sail does not set as well as when using the other methods. The kicking strap cannot be used because the sail is rolled around the boom. One solution is to fit a reefing claw over the rolled sail.

Fig 8.1 Reefing continued

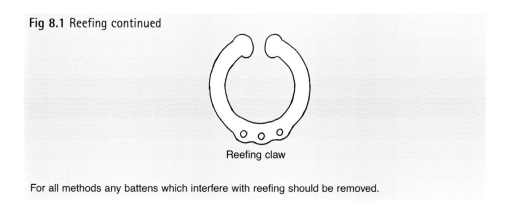

Reefing claw

For all methods any battens which interfere with reefing should be removed.

Lee shore

It is extremely dangerous to sail close to a shore on to which a strong wind is blowing (a *lee shore*). The boat can easily be blown on to it and badly damaged. If your passage involves taking such a risk it is safer to alter your route – and even your destination.

Heavy seas can quickly build up in shallow waters so the skipper may decide to stay out at sea in rough weather rather than risk entering a harbour with an unsheltered approach (such as a lee shore). It is a very difficult decision to make, particularly if the crew are cold, seasick and night is approaching. It is at times like this that the skipper needs the full support of his crew, so it is important that you realise fully the risks involved.

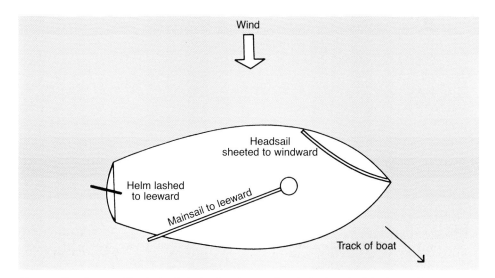

Fig 8.2 Heaving-to. The helm is lashed to leeward and the headsail is sheeted to windward. The drive of the mainsail is thus counteracted.

9 • Special Manoeuvres

Grounding

Going aground on a muddy bottom in fair weather on a rising tide is no emergency; going astern under power and rocking the boat should get you moving again. But going aground on a falling tide can be embarrassing, and you should act quickly to avoid being stuck for several hours. A tow from another boat (if available) is ideal, provided she does not go aground as well. Another option is to launch the dinghy to lay out a kedge anchor, which can be done rapidly by an efficient crew. You then haul on the anchor cable to try to pull the boat clear. With a fin-keeled boat it is sometimes possible to spin the boat around on the keel and use the full power of the engine to get back into deep water.

If the boat is stuck for the duration of the tide, try to ensure that she falls uphill or away from the wind and flood stream. It may be necessary to use an inflatable dinghy as a large fender. A kedge anchor should be laid out into the tidal stream (or wind) ready for pulling off as soon as the boat refloats.

Towing

Receiving a tow

Good communication between the two vessels is essential in this manoeuvre.

The boat which is to be towed should provide the tow line. This should be made fast around the mast, the samson post or a strong cleat, and let out through the foremost fairlead or the anchor roller. (A rag or cloth can be used to reduce chafe.) As the towing vessel approaches, the tow line should be passed across, if necessary by throwing a lighter *heaving line* joined on to the heavier tow line. If the tow is likely to take a long time or the weather is rough, the tow line will have to be long and should be weighted to prevent snatching (snapping taut). To weight the line, use either a length of chain or a heavy weight (such as the anchor) secured to the tow line about half a boat's length ahead of the towed boat. The towed boat should lower its sails and aim to steer directly behind the towing boat.

If accepting a tow from a powerful motor vessel, it is essential that the towing speed is not so fast that the towed boat becomes uncontrollable, or the attachment points are pulled out of the deck. Those in charge of power boats often do not appreciate that sailing boats are not designed to withstand being yanked along at speed like a hooked mackerel.

Giving a tow

It is quite likely that the boat in trouble is undermanned or the crew tired; the boat may also be drifting on to a lee shore. If sea state permits, it is also quite likely that your skipper will want to transfer a crew member to the boat in trouble so that he knows that there is somebody on board who understands what is required. It is often sensible for the towing boat not to lose steerage way, so the crew member (wearing a lifejacket) should be prepared to jump across to the other boat as the skipper steers slowly past. Once on board this crew can help the boat in trouble to get ready to receive a tow.

Once the tow line has been received on board the towing vessel, take a turn around a strong cleat aft. The tow line should be *surged* (eased out slightly) as the strain comes on so that there is no sudden jerk on it. It should be tended throughout the tow and secured so that it can be released immediately, even when under load. A sharp knife should be available in case the line has to be cut in an emergency.

Towing from a quarter cleat sometimes makes it difficult for the towing boat to steer and it may be better to secure a line to both sheet winches which is led aft through the fairleads so that the tow is directly astern.

When the tow is completed, slip the tow line whilst the towed vessel still has sufficient way to reach her berth. The towing vessel should then get clear of the path of the towed boat, as it is possible for the towed boat to overrun the other.

Mooring end on to a quay (Mediterranean moor)

In countries which have little or no tide, boats moor end on to a quay or jetty rather than alongside (Fig 9.1). The easiest way to do this is to head slowly straight for the quay, drop the kedge anchor three boats' lengths off and motor up to the quay using the kedge as a brake. The crew then jump

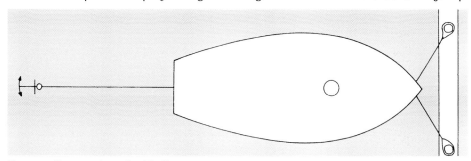

Fig 9.1a First version of a Mediterranean moor.

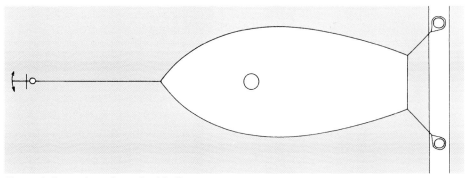

Fig 9.1b Second version of a Mediterranean moor.

ashore with lines. The distance off the quay can then be controlled with the kedge line.

It is, however, more seamanlike to go in astern, dropping the main anchor from the bows. This manoeuvre can be quite difficult unless well practised; it would be prudent, therefore, to anchor three boats' lengths off the quay and then take the lines ashore using the dinghy.

10 • About Ropes

In the past, ropes were made from natural fibres such as cotton, hemp, manila and sisal; today most ropes are made from synthetic fibres such as nylon, polyester and polypropylene. Synthetic ropes are rot-proof, stronger and lighter than natural fibres of the same diameter, but they can be more slippery and difficult to control.

Synthetic rope can be constructed like traditional rope with three strands (cable laid), or it can be plaited or braided (see Fig 10.1). The lay of cable rope is normally right-handed but can be left-handed.

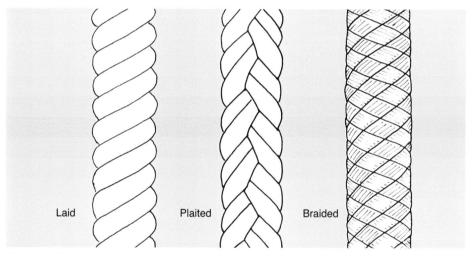

Laid   Plaited   Braided

Fig 10.1 Types of rope.

Nylon is the strongest of the man-made fibres. It stretches and so has good shock-absorbing qualities, making it ideal for an anchor warp or mooring line.

Polyester is almost as strong as nylon but has low stretching properties making it useful for sheets and halyards. (It is available pre-stretched for this purpose.)

Polypropylene is not as strong as nylon or polyester but is lighter and buoyant. It is useful wherever a lightweight floating line is needed, such as a dinghy painter or a line for the lifebuoy.

Care of synthetic ropes

Follow the guidelines below when working with synthetic ropes:

- Wash regularly to remove grit (which can work its way into the rope and cause internal damage) and leave to dry naturally
- Excess heat will cause damage
- Keep away from corrosive chemicals
- Protect from chafe
- Mooring lines should be passed through a piece of hosepipe or bound with rag at the point where they go through a fairlead
- When ropes such as the mainsheet pass around a sheave, the groove in the sheave should be slightly larger than the diameter of the rope
- Halyards or sheets may be turned end for end occasionally to spread wear evenly.

Basic knots, bends and hitches

The term *knot* is generally accepted as meaning any fastening, loop or knob made in cordage. Specifically, a *knot* is a combination of loops used to fasten ropes together or to objects, or to make the end of a rope bigger.

A *bend* is used to join two ropes.

A *hitch* is made up of loops which jam together especially well when under strain but which come apart easily when the strain is removed. Knots, bends and hitches reduce the breaking strain of rope by as much as 50 per cent.

It is advisable to know the correct knot, bend or hitch for any application, and to be able to tie it quickly and efficiently. Failure to do this could result in loss of the boat or even loss of life.

Figs 10.2 to 10.10 show parts of a rope, useful knots, bends and hitches, and some typical applications.

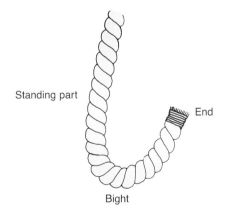

Standing part

End

Bight

Fig 10.2 Parts of a rope.

Finishing off the ends

Unless preventive action is taken, rope ends will eventually fray and the rope will unravel. With synthetic ropes, heat sealing is one answer – apply a hot knife or wire to the end of the rope until the strands melt and fuse together. This

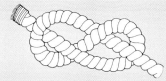

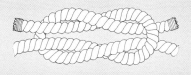

Fig 10.3 Figure of eight, sometimes called a stopper knot. It is used on the end of a sheet to stop it accidentally pulling through a block.

Fig 10.4 Reef knot. Used for fastening two ends of the same rope together when reefing a sail.

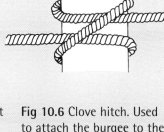

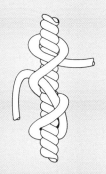

Fig 10.5 Bowline. The best all-purpose knot where a temporary loop is required. Some uses are: to fasten the sheets to the headsail; to join two ropes together; to put a temporary eye in a rope.

Fig 10.6 Clove hitch. Used to attach the burgee to the burgee pole. Unless under equal tension at both ends this hitch will pull out and so it is unsuitable for mooring or for securing fenders permanently.

Fig 10.7 Rolling hitch. Used to fasten a rope to a spar, a chain, or a thicker rope to temporarily take the tension. The direction of pull should be lengthwise across the round turn.

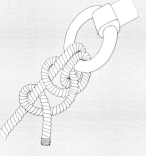

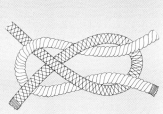

Fig 10.8 Round turn and two half hitches. Used for securing a line to a post or ring or for attaching fenders to the boat. It is secure but easy to undo.

Fig 10.9 Fisherman's bend. For bending a warp on to the ring of an anchor. It is more secure than a round turn and two half hitches, and holds well on slippery rope.

Fig 10.10 Sheet bend. For joining two ropes together. The rope can be passed through twice to make a more secure double sheet bend.

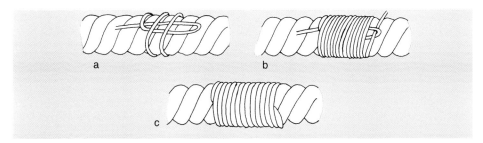

Fig 10.11 Common whipping. This is an easy and quick method of finishing off a rope end.

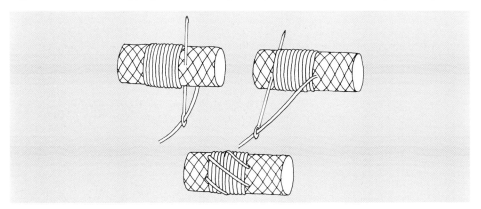

Fig 10.12 Palm and needle whipping. This is more secure than Common Whipping. On braided or plaited rope the stitching stops the whipping slipping out of place when the rope stretches.

does tend to be a temporary rather than a permanent cure however, as the rope *will* fray again. Another method is to heat shrink a plastic sleeve (these are commercially available) on to the end of the rope. Alternatively, weave the end of the rope back into itself to form a back splice (see Fig 10.13), although this inevitably makes the end of the rope thicker, which could prevent it passing through eyes and blocks; this solution is therefore not favoured by some. The most common method is to apply a whipping to the rope end (Figs 10.11 and 10.12), and there are several different methods of doing this.

Splicing

Splicing is a way of making a permanent eye in the rope, finishing the end of a rope, or joining two ropes together.

Cable laid rope (three-strand)
Splicing this type of rope is relatively easy with a little practice. It is a useful skill to have, so that you are able to replce lashings and so on if necessary. Figs 10.13, 10.14 and 10.15 show three basic splices.

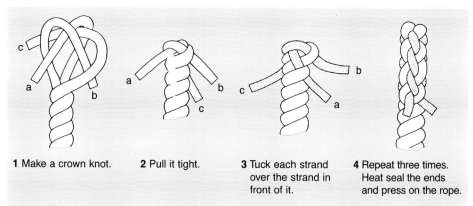

1 Make a crown knot.　　**2** Pull it tight.　　**3** Tuck each strand over the strand in front of it.　　**4** Repeat three times. Heat seal the ends and press on the rope.

Fig 10.13 Back splice. A rope end can be finished in this way to stop it fraying or unravelling but it makes it too bulky to pass through a sheave.

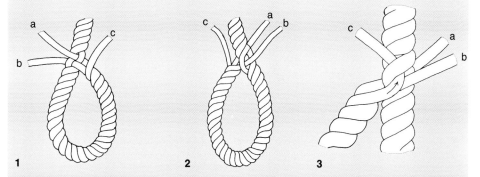

Fig 10.14 Eye splice. This splice is used to put a permanent eye in a rope. (1) Tuck strand (a) under the chosen strand on the standing part of the rope, and strand (b) under the adjacent left-hand strand. (2) Turn the splice over. (3) Tuck strand (c) from right to left under the strand adjacent to the one used for strand (b). (4) Continue as for a back splice until three tucks have been done. (5) Heat seal the ends.

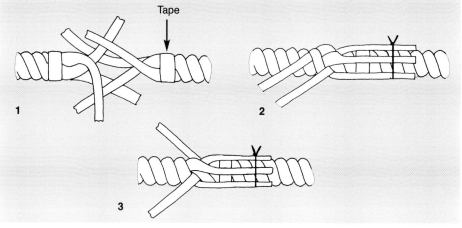

Fig 10.15 Short splice. This splice is used to join two ropes together.

Braided and plaited rope

Plaited rope is more complicated to splice than ordinary three-strand rope. Braided rope has an entirely different construction and special methods using appropriate tools are required for splicing. Not many skippers would expect their crew to be expert in this.

Coiling rope

Ropes are normally coiled before being stowed, when preparing to come alongside or for a heavy line (Figs 10.16 and 10.17).

Winching

A halyard or sheet is turned around a winch drum to take the strain when hoisting or sheeting in a sail. The most important thing to remember when winching is to keep your fingers well away from the winch when there is strain on the rope. The best way to do this is to turn the sheet around the winch drum as shown in the first photograph opposite, clenching your fists

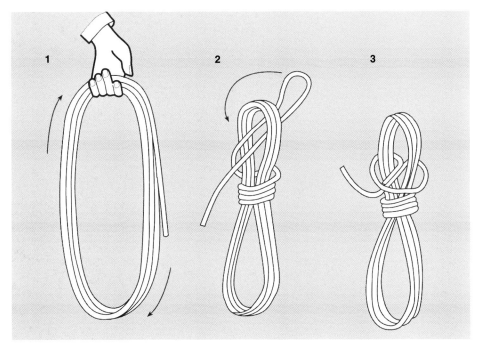

Fig 10.16 Coiling a cable-laid rope. Hold the rope in the left hand and coil in a clockwise direction. A twist at the top of each coil stops the rope twisting. (2) Bind the end around the coils several times and then pass a loop though the coils. (3) Bring the loop back over the top of the coils and push it down to the loops binding the coils. Pull the end tight.

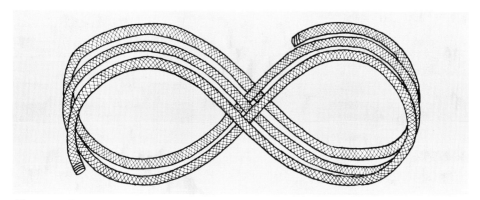

Fig 10.17 Coiling braided or plaited rope. This type of rope twists if coiled as shown for laid rope. It should be coiled in a figure of eight so that the twists cancel out.

Turning a sheet around a winch drum.
Correct – the fists are clenched around the sheet and kept well away from the winch drum.

Wrong – the fingers will be trapped against the winch drum.

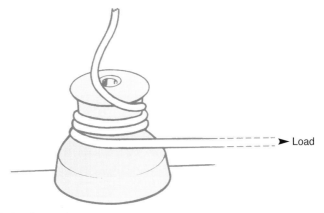

Fig 10.18 Releasing a sheet.

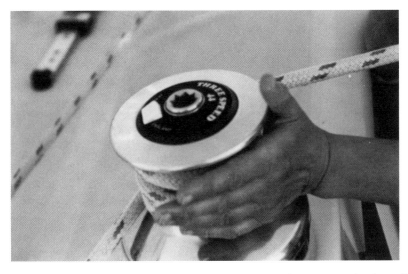

Easing out a sheet. The palm of the hand is placed against the turns on the drum. The end of the sheet is held in the other hand and the sheet gradually eased out.

and keeping them well away from the winch. If the sheet has to be eased out, use the palm of the hand.

To release a sheet, lift it above the winch and pull the turns off the top (Fig 10.18).

A riding turn

Sometimes one turn of a halyard or sheet on the winch drum slips over another and becomes jammed (see photo opposite); this is called a *riding turn*. It may occur because there are too many turns of rope on the winch drum, or because the lead on to or off the winch is not quite right.

A riding turn.

Riding turns usually free themselves, but if hopelessly jammed, attach another line to the halyard or sheet using a rolling hitch (see Fig 10.7) and take the tension on this line. With the load off the winch, it is easy to remove the riding turn from the winch drum.

Making up to a cleat

Fig 10.19 shows how a halyard is secured to a cleat, whilst the top photo overleaf shows a self-jamming cleat, where it is only necessary to turn the rope once around the cleat to secure it. The latter is useful for sheets as it enables them to be released quickly. The other photo on page 60 shows a coiled halyard hung on a cleat.

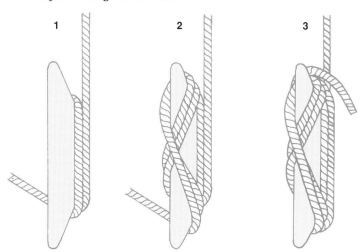

Fig 10.19 Making up to a cleat.
(1) Start with a turn around the cleat. (2) Follow with two or three cross turns.
(3) Finish with a round turn to jam the rope.

A self-jamming cleat.

A coiled halyard hung on a cleat. After cleating a halyard, the remainder is coiled, starting from the end nearest the cleat. About one third of a metre should be left between the cleat and the coil to make a bight in the rope. This is twisted, passed through the coil and looped over the cleat.

Heaving a line

Coil the line and divide the coil into two, holding half in each hand as shown in the photo. Swing half the coil backward and forward, pendulum fashion, and then throw (heave). Allow the other half of the coil to run free until sufficient has run out and the end of the line has reached its target. The end of the line can be made heavier by making a large knot in the end, such as a monkey's fist (Fig 10.20).

Fig 10.20 Monkey's fist. A monkey's fist is made in the end of a rope to make it heavier for heaving. Sometimes it is made around a piece of lead.
(1) Make three loops. (2) Make three more loops outside the first three. (3) Make three final loops over the second three, but inside the first three and splice the end into the standing part.

11 • Weather Wise

At sea it is important to be aware of approaching weather in order to allow appropriate action to be taken in good time. Although there are many ways of obtaining weather forecasts, personal observation and interpretation is still extremely significant.

Personal observations

The ancient mariner's main method of forecasting was to rely on his eyes and the barometer:

Red sky at night, sailor's delight,
Red sky in the morning, sailor's warning.

Trace across the sky a painter's brush,
The winds around you soon will rush.

These sayings may be old, but there is some truth in them. The weather in northern temperate climates tends to move from west to east. A red sky may be caused by dry air containing dust particles; at sunset this foretells a dry day ahead, whilst at sunrise it means the dry air is moving away and possibly taking the fair weather with it.

The appearance of high cloud called cirrus, which looks like wispy threads painted across the sky, often occurs before strong winds and bad weather. The towering cumulus cloud in Fig 11.1 can bring heavy rain and squalls.

Fig 11.1 Cumulus cloud.

The barometer

The barometer measures atmospheric pressure; changes in barometric pressure can forewarn of forthcoming changes in the weather.

The barometric presssure range is normally from a low of 960 millibars to a high of 1040 millibars, the mean being 1000 millibars (*one standard atmospheric pressure*). Generally, the higher the pressure the more settled the weather; the lower the pressure the more unsettled. Rapidly changing readings of barometric pressure warn of significant changes and probable high winds.

Rising rapidly – initially better weather, but it may not be long lasting.
Falling rapidly – bad weather and gales not far off.
Rising steadily – a sign of good weather.
Falling steadily – a sign of bad weather.

So there is also some truth in the following rhyme:

*When the glass falls low
Prepare for a blow.
When it slowly rises high,
Lofty canvas you may fly.*

Wind

Changes in pressure can result from temperature differences in adjacent regions. Warm air rises causing a low pressure area on the earth's surface; cold air descends causing a high pressure on the earth's surface. Air tends to flow from a high pressure area to a low pressure area and this movement of air creates wind. Wind force is measured on a scale known as the *Beaufort scale*, part of which is shown overleaf.

Services available

You may frequently be asked to obtain the latest weather forecast. Generally, the following services are available.

British Broadcasting Corporation
• *The Shipping Forecast*
The Shipping Forecast is broadcast by the BBC on Long Wave (LW) on a frequency of 198 kHz (equivalent to a wavelength of 1215 metres) and also on Radio 4 FM services. It is broadcast four times a day at 0048 (LW and FM), 0535 (LW and FM). 1201 (LW only), and 1754 (LW only from Monday to Friday and LW and FM on Saturday and Sunday).

Beaufort Wind Scale

No.	Description	Limit of mean wind speed (knots)	Appearance	Approx. wave height (metres)
0	Calm	Less than 1	Sea like a mirror.	0
1	Light airs	1 to 3	Ripples like scales.	Less than 0.1
2	Light breeze	4 to 6	Small wavelets. Crests have a glassy appearance but do not break.	0.1 to 0.3
3	Gentle breeze	7 to 10	Large wavelets. A few white horses.	0.3 to 0.9
4	Moderate breeze	11 to 16	Small waves becoming longer. Frequent white horses.	0.9 to 1.5
5	Fresh breeze	17 to 21	Moderate waves. Many white horses.	1.5 to 2.5
6	Strong breeze	22 to 27	Large waves. White foam crests. Some spray.	2.5 to 4
7	Near gale	28 to 33	Sea heaps up. Waves break. Streaks of foam.	4 to 6
8	Gale	34 to 40	Moderately high waves of greater length. Crests breaking into spindrift. Extensive streaks of foam.	6 to 8

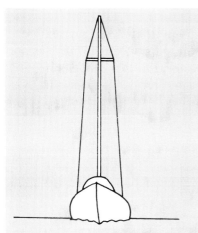

Beaufort force 0: The boat is motoring.

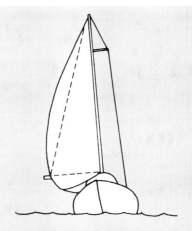

Beaufort force 3: The boat is sailing with a large genoa and full mainsail.

Beaufort force 5: The boat sails well with a working staysail and full mainsail.

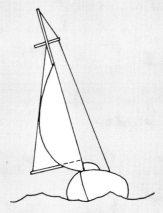

Beaufort force 7: The boat sails with a storm jib and reefed mainsail.

Beaufort force 8: The boat runs with only a storm jib.

Fig 11.2 How the boat responds to different wind strengths.

This forecast gives gale warnings, a general synopsis giving the position and movement of pressure systems, and a 24-hour forecast for sea areas. The broadcasts at 0048 and 0535 include reports from coastal stations and the forecast for 24 hours ahead for inshore waters (up to 12 miles offshore).

It is a good idea to listen to these broadcasts from time to time in order to become familiar with the terms and format. Some of the terms are explained below.

• *Gale warnings*
The BBC broadcasts gale warnings for shipping forecast areas on Radio 4 at the first available programme juncture after receipt.

Shipping Forecast Terms

Length of time when a gale warning is expected

Imminent	= within 6 hours
Soon	= between 6 and 12 hours
Later	= between 12 and 24 hours

Movement of systems

Slowly	= less than 15 knots
Steadily	= 15 to 25 knots
Rather quickly	= 25 to 35 knots
Rapidly	= 35 to 45 knots
Very rapidly	= more than 45 knots

Pressure changes

Slowly	= <1.5 mb in 3 hours
Quickly	= 3.6 mb to 6 mb within 3 hours
Very Rapidly	= >6 mb in 3 hours

Visibility

Very good	= more than 30 miles
Good	= 5 to 30 miles
Moderate	= 2 to 5 miles
Poor	= less than 2 miles
Mist or Haze	= between 1000 and 2000 metres (1100 to 2200 yards)
Fog	= less than 1000 metres (1100 yards)
Thick fog	= less than 366 metres (400 yards)

• Land forecasts

These are broadcast at various times on Radio 4 and, used with the shipping forecast, give useful background information.

• Leisure users forecast

A special forecast for the leisure user is broadcast on Radio 4 at 0556 on Saturdays and at 0542 on Sundays.

Other sources

• Local radio

Many local radio stations broadcast weather information for nearby coastal waters.

• Coast radio stations

Coast radio stations are operated by British Telecom. They repeat the relevant part of the BBC Shipping Forecast for local sea areas, including gale warnings, on VHF radio.

• HM Coastguard

The local inshore waters forecast is broadcast by the coastguard every 4 hours. Strong Wind Warnings are also broadcast if the wind is expected to reach force 6 or more up to 5 miles offshore. These broadcasts are announced on VHF channel 16 and then broadcast on channel 67.

• Marinecall Select

This service offers forecasts and coastal reports by telephone and is normally updated hourly.

• Metcall Direct

This service offers direct access to a forecaster via telephone, either from the UK or the Continent.

• Internet

The Met Office has a website called Metweb (*www.met-office.gov.uk*). Products include: weather charts, 2, 3 and 5 day forecasts, satellite pictures, shipping forecasts, gale warnings and coastal reports.

• Navtex

Navtex is an international automated direct printing service broadcast on a radio frequency of 518 kHz. Transmissions include navigation warnings and weather forecasts.

• *Radiofax*

Weather charts are available via radiofacsimile broadcasts.

• *Newspapers and television*

Surface pressure charts are often printed in newspapers or shown on television. These are a useful guide to general weather trends but need to be used in conjunction with other information.

• *Local sources*

Useful information about the weather for a particular area can be found out from local sources such as fishermen, yacht clubs, harbourmasters and marina staff.

Details of forecasts

Details of times of weather forecasts and reports can be found in newspapers, nautical almanacs and in the *Admiralty List of Radio Signals Vol. 5*. Times and details of forecasts do change so these sources should be checked regularly.

12 · Steering a Course

When there are no suitable landmarks a compass is used to steer the boat on the correct course.

Compasses

Liquid-filled compass

The compass may be liquid-filled with a card graduated through 360° and suspended on a pivot. Magnets attached to the card ensure that the north graduation always indicates the magnetic north pole. There is a line on the casing called a lubber line which corresponds with the fore-and-aft line of the boat. See photo, right.

A surface-mounted card type compass.
Photo: Yachting Instruments Ltd.

Electronic Compass

An electronic compass has a digital display connected to a remote sensor. The sensor can also provide information to other instruments. See photos.

The DataScope shown is an electronic digital compass for taking bearings. It also has a range finder and a chronometer.

Steering a course

When the desired course is lined up with the *lubber line* of a liquid-filled compass or shown on the digital display of an electronic compass, the boat is heading in the direction indicated.

Steering an accurate compass course is not easy, especially in rough weather, and initially it is easier to learn whilst under power. Experiment with the helm, moving it slightly and observing which way the figures on the display appear to move. The figures do not in fact move; the compass always indicates magnetic north and the boat swings around. Dependent upon the compass display, which may only be marked every 5 degrees, it is often easier to steer to the nearest graduation rather than try to estimate a degree or two between.

Do not forget to look up frequently to see what is around the boat.

Influences on the compass

The earth resembles a large magnet, with a magnetic field, magnetic meridians and a magnetic north and south pole. The magnetic poles do not coincide with the true geographical poles. The angle between a magnetic meridian and a true meridian is called *variation* (Fig 12.1). Variation can be either west or east and when applied to the charted course it results in what is known as a *magnetic course*, indicated by the letter 'M' placed after the figures: 148°M. When correcting a true course to a magnetic course, westerly variation is added and easterly variation subtracted:

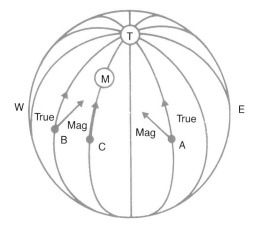

Fig 12.1 Variation. Magnetic north M is offset slightly from true north T, so the variation between the two will depend on where you are on the earth's surface in relation to them. At point B variation is east, at A it is west, whilst at C the variation is nil since true and magnetic north are directly in line.

Example

True course	142° T +
Variation 6° west	6
Magnetic course	148° M

Fig 12.2 Compass rose.

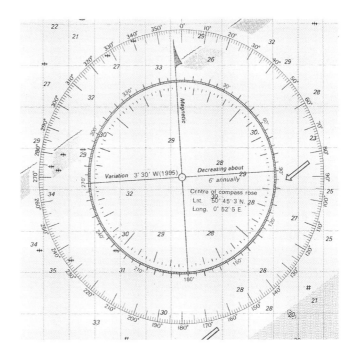

Variation is printed vertically on the compass rose (Fig 12.2). On the compass rose the variation is 3°30'W for 1995 decreasing 6' annually. For 2001 the variation will be 3°00'W.

Deviation – the influence of the boat's magnetic field

The steering compass can be affected by ferrous metals, live electrical systems and any equipment containing a magnet, so it is important to site the compass as far away from these influences as possible. The effect on the compass of these influences is called *deviation*.

Deviation alters with different headings of the boat and so a table is necessary to show the relevant correction to apply.

One way of making up a deviation table is to use landmarks. When two known landmarks are seen to be in line from the boat, they are said to be in *transit*. If the boat is sailed across this transit on a variety of *headings*, deviation can be determined for each heading. As the boat crosses the transit, note the compass bearing of the transit and the heading of the boat using the steering compass. (On most small boats a special attachment called an azimuth ring is needed to enable the steering compass to be used for taking accurate bearings.) Compare the compass bearing of the transit with the magnetic bearing of the transit (found by applying the local variation to the true bearing obtained from the chart). The difference between the two is the deviation for that course.

Deviation can deflect the compass needle to the west or to the east. When applied to a magnetic course to find the compass course to steer, westerly deviation is added and easterly deviation subtracted:

Example

Magnetic course	148° M –
Deviation 5° East	5°
Compass course	143° C

A compass course is indicated by the letter 'C' placed after the figures, for example 143°C.

Temporary deviation can be caused on any magnetic compass by the close proximity of metal objects such as beer cans, penknives, tools and so forth. Always be alert to this danger and keep these objects well away from the compass.

Taking bearings

A hand-held magnetic compass is used to find the direction of an object on the shore (a landmark) from the boat. This direction is known as a *bearing*. A *hand-bearing compass* will not be subject to any deviation provided it is held well away from any object on the boat which might exert a magnetic influence. It will, however, still be subject to variation.

To take the bearing of a landmark, hold the compass firmly and align the 'v' sight with the landmark. When the card stops swinging, note the figure under the line on the compass or under the 'v'-shaped sight: this is the magnetic bearing of the landmark from the boat (see Fig 12.3).

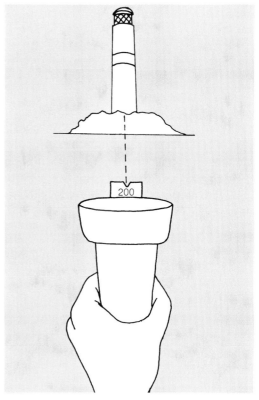

Fig 12.3 To take a bearing align the 'V' sight with the landmark.

Taking a bearing with the hand-bearing compass. Photo: David Williams.

The photo shows a mini hand-bearing compass which is held level with the eye. The object is sighted over the edge of the compass above a prism which shows its bearings.

It is difficult to get an accurate bearing on a rolling or pitching boat as the compass card is very sensitive to movement. The rougher the weather, the more inaccurate the bearing is likely to be. If several bearings are to be taken, those abeam will alter more rapidly than those ahead or astern so they should be taken last.

Always note the time at which bearings are taken, and the log reading if appropriate.

13 • Finding the Way

A chart is a nautical map, a pilot (also called sailing directions) is a book giving detailed information about harbours, anchorages, the coastline, tidal conditions, local weather patterns and so forth. You will use both when navigating a course.

The theory of coastal navigation, such as plotting on the chart, can be learned on a shorebased course over the winter. It is useful to have an understanding of pilotage – navigating with the use of floating marks (buoys) or other land features such as lighthouses, beacons, towers or churches, where the next mark on the passage can be seen at all times. It is essential to recognise the various marks both by day and by night, and be able to locate their positions on a chart.

Buoyage

The system of buoyage around North-West Europe has been developed by the International Association of Lighthouse Authorities and is called IALA System A. (IALA System B applies around North America.)

Lateral marks

A lateral mark indicates the port or starboard side of a channel when used in relation to the Conventional Direction of Buoyage. The Conventional Direction of Buoyage (which is shown by a broad arrow on large-scale Admiralty charts) is usually in a clockwise direction around land masses, or in the general direction of approach from seaward when entering a harbour, river or estuary (Fig 13.1).

When proceeding in this direction, pass red cylindrical marks to port (left) and green conical marks to starboard (right). Their shapes may vary (see Figs 13.2 and 13.3). Lateral marks do not always carry topmarks.

Where the channel divides, the lateral marks are modified by a green or red horizontal band which indicates the main or preferred channel (Figs 13.4 and 13.5).

Cardinal marks

Cardinal marks are pillar shaped, with black and yellow horizontal bands and black topmarks. They are placed north, south, east or west of the danger that they mark. It is easy to remember which mark you are looking at (you have to know to which side of it to go) if you note that the topmarks point

Fig 13.1 The conventional direction of buoyage in the British Isles follows the arrows shown.

upwards for the north mark, downwards for the south mark, make an egg shape for the east mark, and a wineglass shape for the west mark. If you cannot see the topmark properly, the placing of the black band corresponds to the way the topmarks point. As for the lights, the number of flashes corresponds to the mark's 'clockface' position (see Figs 13.6 and 13.7).

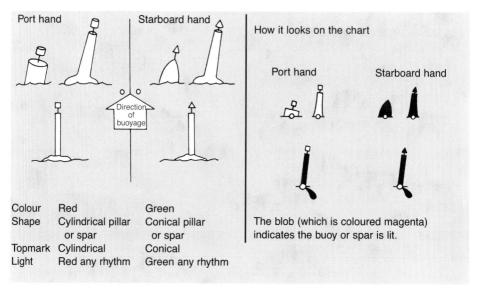

Fig 13.2 Lateral marks.

Fig 13.3 When entering a harbour the red port-hand marks are left to port and the green starboard-hand marks are left to starboard.

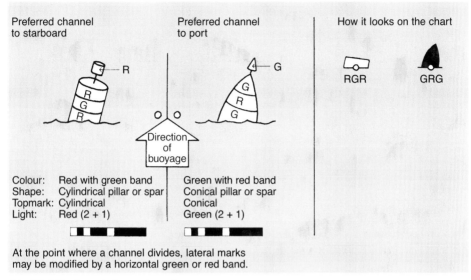

Preferred channel to starboard | Preferred channel to port | How it looks on the chart

— R   — G

RGR   GRG

Direction of buoyage

Colour: Red with green band   Green with red band
Shape: Cylindrical pillar or spar   Conical pillar or spar
Topmark: Cylindrical   Conical
Light: Red (2 + 1)   Green (2 + 1)

At the point where a channel divides, lateral marks
may be modified by a horizontal green or red band.

Fig 13.4 Preferred channel marks.

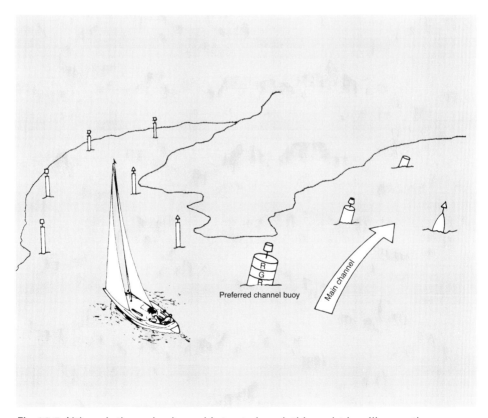

Preferred channel buoy

Main channel

Fig 13.5 Although the main channel is to starboard, this yacht is sailing up the
secondary channel to her mooring up the creek.

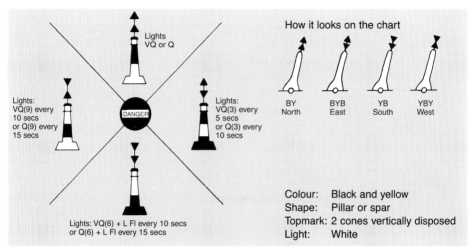

Fig 13.6 Cardinal marks. These marks are positioned to the north, east, south or west of danger.

Fig 13.7 A cardinal mark. The boat is passing to the *south* of the south cardinal mark to avoid the rock to the north of the mark.

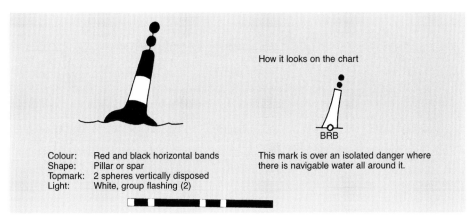

Colour: Red and black horizontal bands
Shape: Pillar or spar
Topmark: 2 spheres vertically disposed
Light: White, group flashing (2)

How it looks on the chart

BRB

This mark is over an isolated danger where there is navigable water all around it.

Fig 13.8 Isolated danger mark.

Isolated danger marks
Figure 13.8 shows an isolated danger mark which is placed immediately over an underwater obstruction.

Safe water marks
A safe water mark indicates safe water all around it. It may be used as a landfall mark or a mid-channel mark (Fig 13.9).

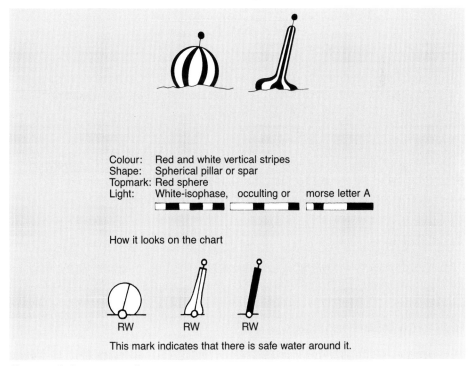

Colour: Red and white vertical stripes
Shape: Spherical pillar or spar
Topmark: Red sphere
Light: White-isophase,   occulting or   morse letter A

How it looks on the chart

RW   RW   RW

This mark indicates that there is safe water around it.

Fig 13.9 Safe water mark.

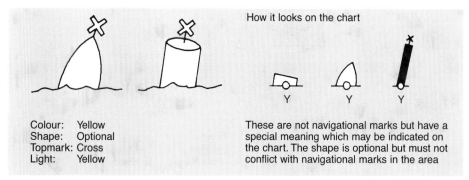

Colour: Yellow
Shape: Optional
Topmark: Cross
Light: Yellow

How it looks on the chart

These are not navigational marks but have a special meaning which may be indicated on the chart. The shape is optional but must not conflict with navigational marks in the area

Fig 13.10 Special marks.

Special marks

A special mark has no navigational significance, but indicates a special feature such as a traffic separation scheme, spoil grounds, or a military exercise area (Fig 13.10).

Shore lights

In addition to buoys, lighthouses and beacons on the shore are used to determine the boat's position by day; or by night when they are identified by lights with specific characteristics.

Light characteristics

Lights used for navigation operate on a regular cyclic period during which they display specific identification characteristics. Fig 13.11 shows some light characteristics; Fig 13.12 shows sectored lights.

The time in seconds that a light takes to display its complete characteristics, which includes the time that it is eclipsed, is called the *period*.

It is a good idea, when trying to identify a light, to use a stopwatch to time the period. It is easy to imagine that the characteristics match those of an expected light and thus make a wrong identification.

Transits

Two shore objects or lights in line are often used to navigate safe entry to a harbour or river. Such marks are called leading marks or transits (Fig 13.13)

Clearing bearings

Sometimes specific bearings or transits are used to make sure that the boat stays in a safe area (Fig 13.14).

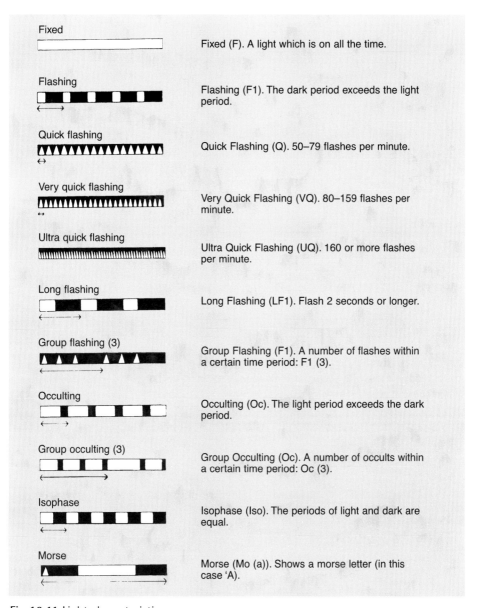

Fig 13.11 Light characteristics

Withies

Further up a river or creek, the navigational marks may consist only of tree branches or sticks stuck into the mud, marking the edges of the navigable channel. These are called *withies*, and are not painted any colour (see Fig 13.15).

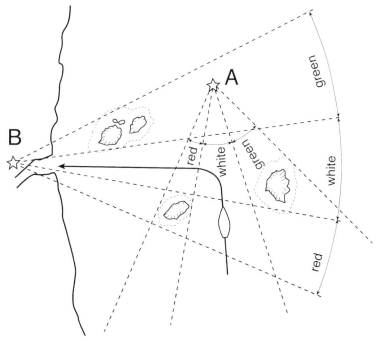

Fig 13.12 Sectored lights. Many lights have sectors of different colour: here the vessel must keep in the white sector of light A until she reaches the white sector of light B, when she can turn to port.

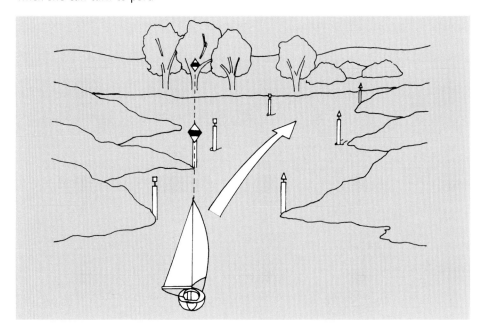

Fig 13.13 A transit. The boat lines up the diamonds to enter the river and then keeps between the port and starboard marks.

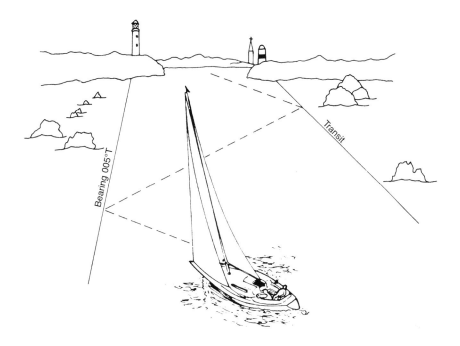

Fig 13.14 Clearing bearings. The boat uses clearing bearings to stay in safe water. She alters course when the church and the beacon are in transit.

Fig 13.15 Withies. Further up the river, tree branches may be stuck in the mud to mark the edge of the channel. These are called withies.

14 ● Who Goes First?

Just as there is a highway code to ensure the safety of road users, so there are rules to ensure the safety of seafarers – the International Regulations For Preventing Collision At Sea. You should have a thorough knowledge of the principal rules and at least a working knowledge of the remainder. Those concerning small sailing and power driven vessels are discussed below but a full copy of the rules should be studied in conjunction with this chapter.

Keeping a good lookout

This is probably the most important rule because collisions cannot be avoided unless the danger of collision has been observed. Make sure a proper lookout is kept *at all times*, not only watching but listening, especially if visibility is poor. In a sailing boat which is heeling over, the crew

Fig **14.1** Keep a good lookout especially to leeward.

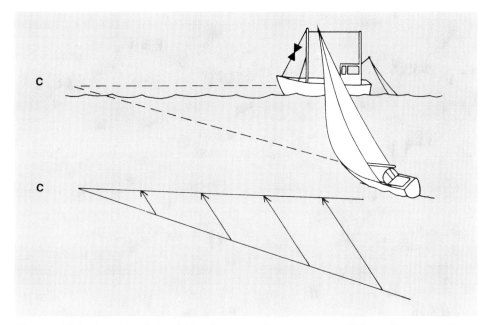

Fig 14.2 If the bearing of the fishing boat remains constant, collision will occur at C.

must be particularly observant to leeward as the headsail can obscure the helmsman's vision in this direction (Fig 14.1).

Is there a risk of collision?

Take a compass bearing of any boat that you suspect is on a collision course. Take further bearings at regular intervals and if there is little or no difference between them, a risk of collision is deemed to exist (see Fig 14.2).

Avoiding action

Avoiding action should be: a *positive* alteration of course made in ample time and with due observance of the rules of good seamanship. A positive alteration of course is about 40 degrees; ample time (for a sailing boat) is about 5 minutes; good seamanship is not crossing ahead of another vessel. Always travel at a safe speed relative to the prevailing weather conditions and traffic density, so that action can be taken in good time to avoid a collision. This may mean slowing down if there is bad visibility or when other boats are in close proximity, or speeding up (by using the engine) if there is little or no wind near a harbour entrance or in a shipping lane (a sailing boat is required to start its engine if travelling at less than 3 knots when crossing a shipping lane).

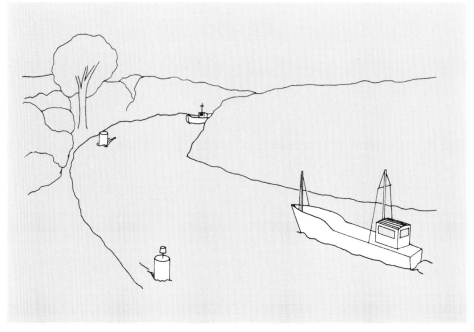

Fig 14.3 Approaching the bend in the river, sound one long blast and listen.

Narrow channels

In narrow channels, keep over to the side of the channel which is to your starboard. Sailing boats and boats of less than 20 metres in length must not impede the passage of a vessel using the channel which can only navigate within that channel. If there is sufficient depth of water outside the main channel the smaller boat should stay out of that channel. Always cross the channel at right angles.

When approaching a bend in a river which obstructs a clear view, sound one long blast on a siren or foghorn and listen for a reply (Fig 14.3).

Do not anchor the boat near or in a channel.

Crossing a traffic separation scheme

Around headlands or in channels where there is a lot of shipping, larger vessels are confined to special traffic lanes which are marked on the chart. Again, if you have to cross a traffic lane, do so at right angles and as quickly as possible (Fig 14.4). When crossing, it is the heading of the boat that should be at right angles to the traffic lanes, and not the ground track (which will be affected by any tidal stream).

There are also inshore traffic zones which may be used by small craft.

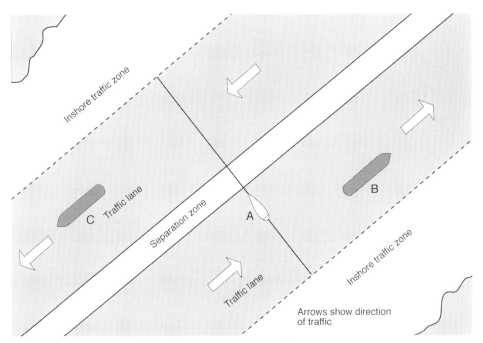

Fig 14.4 Crossing shipping lanes. Boat A must cross as quickly as possible at right angles to the vessels using the traffic lanes (boats B and C).

Additional rules to know

Illustrated in the following figures are: rules for sailing boats (Fig 14.5), rules for boats under power (Fig 14.6), the overtaking rule (Fig 14.7), lights, shapes and fog signals (Figs 14.8 to 14.10), and rules for smaller boats (Fig 14.11).

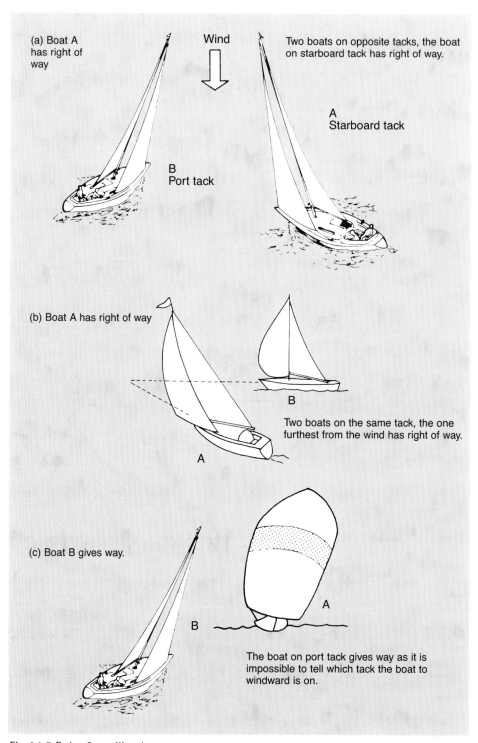

(a) Boat A has right of way

Wind

Two boats on opposite tacks, the boat on starboard tack has right of way.

A
Starboard tack

B
Port tack

(b) Boat A has right of way

B

Two boats on the same tack, the one furthest from the wind has right of way.

A

(c) Boat B gives way.

B

A

The boat on port tack gives way as it is impossible to tell which tack the boat to windward is on.

Fig 14.5 Rules for sailing boats.

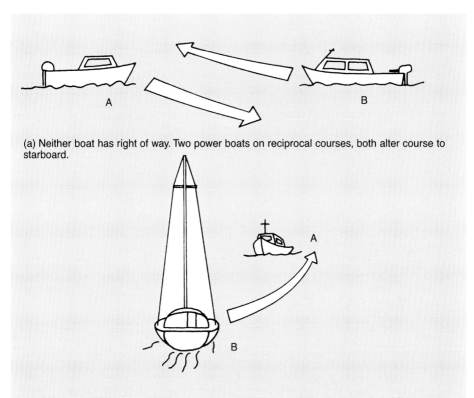

(a) Neither boat has right of way. Two power boats on reciprocal courses, both alter course to starboard.

(b) Boat A has right of way. Two boats under power, the one which has the other on her starboad side keeps clear.

Fig 14.6 Rules for boats under power.

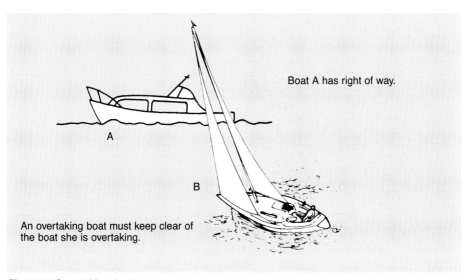

Boat A has right of way.

An overtaking boat must keep clear of the boat she is overtaking.

Fig 14.7 Overtaking boat.

Lights, shapes and fog signals

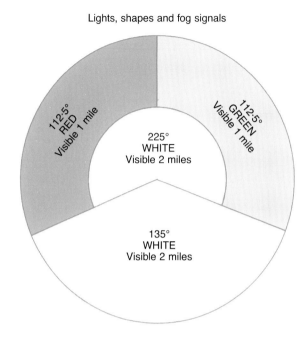

Fig 14.8 Arc and visibility of lights for a boat of less than 12 metres in length.

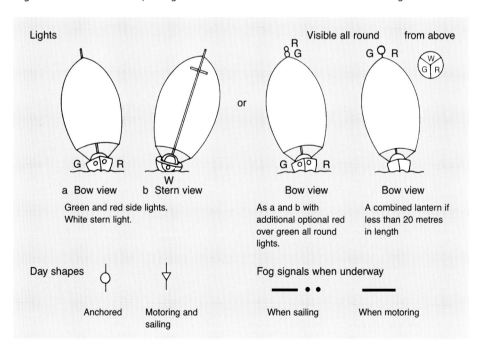

Fig 14.9 A sailing boat.

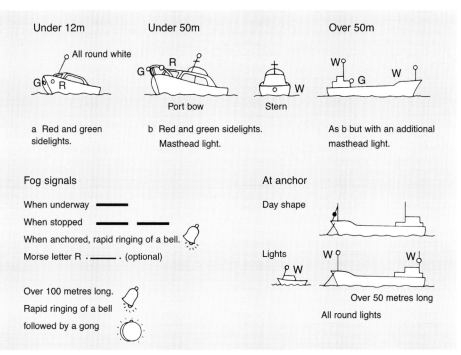

Fig 14.10 A power-driven boat.

A boat under power of less than seven metres may show just an all round white light if it is not practicable to show side lights.

A sailing boat of less than seven metres or a boat being rowed should have a torch ready to exhibit when required.

Fig 14.11 Smaller boats.

Sound signals used when vessels
are in sight of one another

•	One short blast	I am altering course to starboard
••	Two short blasts	I am altering course to port
•••	Three short blasts	My engines are going astern
•••••	Five short blasts	I am unsure of your intentions
•••• •	Four short blasts followed by one short blast	I intend to turn completely around to starboard
•••• ••	Four short blasts followed by two short blasts	I intend to turn completely around to port
— — •	Two long blasts followed by one short blast	I wish to overtake you on your starboard side
— — ••	Two long blasts followed by two short blasts	I wish to overtake you on your port side
— • — •	One long blast, one short blast, one long blast, one short blast	You may overtake me on the side indicated.

15 • Courtesy Costs Nothing

It is always a pleasure to be a member of the crew of a smart boat. This impression of 'smartness' is created by both smooth execution of manoeuvres, and observance of the rules of etiquette and courtesy.

Flag etiquette

A cruising boat is 'properly dressed' when flying a masthead burgee and her national ensign.

The burgee
The burgee is usually that of a club or association of which the skipper is a member, and is flown at all times when the boat is in commission with the skipper on board or absent for a period of no longer than 24 hours.

The ensign
The ensign is normally red; blue or white ensigns can be worn only if authorised by special warrant. At sea, the ensign is worn at all times; in harbour it is hoisted at 0800 in summer and 0900 in winter, and lowered at sunset or 2100, whichever is earlier. When passing a warship of any nationality it is courteous to dip the ensign by lowering it until the warship responds by dipping and hoisting hers. The ensign is not worn when racing.

The courtesy ensign
When visiting a foreign country, the ensign of that country should be flown from the starboard spreader for the entire duration of your stay in territorial waters. This is known as a courtesy ensign.

House flag
This is a rectangular flag with a design personal to the owner, the house flag is flown from the starboard spreader under the same circumstances as the burgee. If you need to fly a courtesy ensign from the starboard spreader, the house flag is flown on the port spreader.

International code flags
These may be flown to indicate their code meanings on the starboard spreader or, if this is already occupied, from the port spreader. The most common flags are shown in the table overleaf.

International Code Flags

	Description		Meaning
Flag Q	*shape*:	rectangular	Boat requesting customs
	colour:	yellow	clearance
Flag A	*shape*:	swallow tail	Diver operating
	colour:	blue and white	
Flag B	*shape*:	swallow tail	Carrying, loading or
	colour:	red	unloading a dangerous cargo
Flag R over	*shape*:	rectangular (both)	
Flag Y	*colour* R:	yellow cross on a red ground	Keep well clear and go at slow speed when
	colour Y:	red and yellow diagonal stripes	passing me
Flag N over	*shape*:	rectangular (both)	
Flag C	N *colour*:	blue and white chequered	
	C *colour*:	red horizontal band with a white horizontal band each side on a blue ground	International distress signal

Dressing a boat overall

On special occasions when in harbour, international code flags are hoisted from the stem to the masthead(s) and back to the stern. The boat is then 'dressed overall'.

Behaviour in port

When berthing alongside another boat, if anyone is on board it is normal to ask if you may come alongside. You should provide your own fenders and not rely upon the other boat to do so.

If other boats have to be crossed to get ashore, this should be done by passing over their foredeck and not across the cockpit, making as little noise as possible, especially late at night. On first crossing a boat, again ask permission to do so. Try to tread as lightly as possible, and do not put weight or pressure on fittings which look inadequate.

Pollution

Keeping the environment clean is a responsibility that applies to all yachtsmen.

Retain all litter on board for disposal when you next arrive at a marina; do not ditch anything within six miles of the shore, and beyond that only dispose of biodegradable waste

In some countries it is obligatory for all craft to have a sewage holding tank which can be emptied and flushed in the harbour. Double check the relevant regulations before embarking on your trip.

16 • Engines

Diesel engines

Most small boat inboard engines are diesel. They do not have ignition and spark plugs like petrol engines and can therefore run without a battery. They usually incorporate a flywheel which has to be rotated rapidly (either by hand or with an electric motor) to start. For cold starting there is either a decompression lever, which is kept up or off until the flywheel is rotating fast enough and then pushed down; or a pre-heater which is switched on for about 20 seconds before rotating the flywheel.

Once a diesel engine is running, keep it running fairly fast and under load. It will give full power as soon as it is started without needing to warm up. When starting from cold, it should not be run for short intervals and then stopped.

To stop a diesel engine there is usually a special spring-operated stop lever, or sometimes an electrically operated switch.

The main problem that may arise with a diesel engine is fuel contamination, so clear any water or dirt accumulated in the fuel. Most water comes from condensation in fuel tanks left nearly empty in cold weather. If water does get into the fuel it is normally trapped in a water separator which can be emptied of water and dirt by opening its drain plug. If water gets beyond the water separator, it has to be removed by bleeding the fuel system – not a difficult job in harbour but quite tricky at sea.

Petrol engines

These suffer similar problems to petrol engines in cars. Spark plugs must be kept clean and dry and the gaps correctly set. Petrol is a volatile liquid with a lower flash point than diesel and so any leaks are more dangerous and constitute a fire risk.

Daily checks

All engines react badly to sea water so they must be kept clean and dry. If an engine has been immersed in salt water, wash it thoroughly with fresh water and dry it out as soon as possible.

Inboard engine

- Check the oil level in the engine and the gear box.
- Check for oil and fuel leaks.
- Check for water in the fuel.
- See that the batteries are charged.
- Check the fuel level.
- Check that the cooling water seacock is open if the engine is going to be used.
- If cooled by sea water check that it is circulating properly.
- If cooled by fresh water see that the water tank is full.

Outboard engine

- See that the fuel tank and the spare fuel can are both full.
- Check that the sparking plugs are clean and the gaps correctly set.
- Carry spare sparking plugs and a plug spanner.
- Keep the bearings greased.
- See that the correct oil/petrol mixture is used.
- When running check that the cooling water is circulating by watching the outlet.
- When it has finished running, run fresh water through the cooling system if possible then thoroughly dry the outside of the engine.

17 • Emergencies

Man overboard

It is important that each member of the crew can take the helm and get the boat back to a person who has fallen overboard. The method used to bring the boat back alongside the person will depend upon:

- The experience of the helmsman
- Weather conditions
- Visibility
- The type of boat. A novice may only be able to perform this manoeuvre under power, and if the engine is serviceable there is no reason why it should not be used. However, in case of engine failure it is necessary to know and practise at least one other method of bringing the boat back under sail, and a good skipper will train his crew accordingly, practising with a fender or other floating object. *Do not practise the man overboard drill by asking a member of the crew to jump into the water.*

Four methods of recovery are described below. Whichever is used, the objective is to get back to the person quickly and stop the boat alongside him. In cold water, survival time is counted in minutes not hours. The routine described in the box opposite applies to all methods.

Method 1: sailing
Whatever point of sailing the boat is on, immediately go on to a reach and sail a sufficient distance away (5 to 7 boat lengths) from the person in the water to enable the boat to reverse course and return under full control. When the boat is ready, tack round on to the opposite reach and sail back along the previous track. Make the final approach on a fine reach with both sails flying so that the boat can be stopped with the person to leeward ready for the pick up.

Using this method, the boat is fully under control and the crew have time to organise themselves, but it does require a certain amount of sailing skill and also takes the boat a distance away from the person in the water.

Method 2: sailing
When running in light airs or if only a headsail is set, this method is preferable and the boat may be gybed round. However, if the winds are strong or the helmsman inexperienced, damage to the boat and possibly a

Man overboard

• • • • •

1 As soon as someone falls overboard shout 'man overboard' to alert all the crew.

2 Throw the lifebuoy (and the dan buoy, if carried) into the water, activating the light if at night.

3 Point continuously towards the person in the water, calling out his relative position and distance off. Do not take your eyes off him. In a rough sea or at night he can be lost to view very quickly.

4 It is a good idea to throw in other floating objects periodically so that a trail is left which can be followed when the boat turns round and heads back.

5 If a spinnaker is set, course should be altered towards the wind and the spinnaker lowered behind the mainsail, stowing it in the cabin out of the way. Similarly, if the engine is to be used, the mainsail should be lowered.

6 Check that no lines are trailing over the side which could snag around the propeller.

7 Make a note of the time, the course and log reading in case the person is lost to sight and it is necessary to retrace the boat's track.

further accident may occur. This method does require the helmsman to have a good knowledge of the boat's handling capabilities.

Method 3: sailing boat under power

Immediately heave-to and start the engine. Lower the sails and secure or, if shorthanded, drop the mainsail and let the headsail fly. Make sure no sheets are trailing in the water. This method is within the capabilties of an inexperienced crew provided they have been shown how to heave-to. When the boat reaches the person in the water and he is secured, the engine must be stopped to avoid possible injury from the propeller.

Method 4: power boat

Steer the propeller away from the person in the water by altering course towards the side over which he has fallen. Turn a tight circle to come up alongside, with the boat head to wind.

The pick-up

It is extremely difficult to lift a waterlogged person out of the water, especially if he is unconscious. Whilst the boat is returning to the casualty,

The liferaft

It is extremely important that everyone on board knows how to launch, inflate and board the liferaft.

Do not launch the liferaft until you are ready to use it as it may capsize.

Do not abandon the boat if it is still afloat however; it is a bigger target for the rescue services and it is also more stable than the liferaft.

Before abandoning

1 Send out a distress call giving your position
2 Don plenty of warm clothing and foul weather gear. Don lifejackets
3 It is very useful to keep a grab bag ready and useful items such as a mirror for signalling, torch, spare plastic bottles of water etc.
4 If available, take the EPIRB into the liferaft with you.

Launching

1 Make sure the painter is secured to a strong point
2 Release the fastenings which secure the liferaft to the boat and launch it, keeping clear of the painter
3 When it is in the water, pull in the slack on the painter and then give a sharp tug. This should inflate the liferaft.

Boarding

1 Do not jump on or into the liferaft but board from a ladder or from the sea, getting the heaviest and strongest person in first
2 Once fully boarded, cut painter and paddle clear of boat.

Procedure on the liferaft

1 Stream the drogue
2 Elect a leader
3 Open the survival pack and take out the first aid kit, pyrotechnics and seasickness tablets. Make sure you seal the survival pack after use.
4 Issue seasickness tablets
5 Check for leaks
6 Treat any injuries
7 Do not issue water for the first 24 hours unless to an injured person losing blood
8 Do not drink sea water or urine
9 Keep warm
10 Post a look-out and try to estimate your position
11 Activate the EPIRB.

prepare a line with a bowline in the end. Secure the free end to the boat and place the loop either over the man's head to fit around his waist, or he can put his foot into it and use it as a ladder. If a boarding ladder is available this should be used. A lifebelt (or quoit) with a light floating line attached should be available to throw to the person if the helmsman misjudges the final approach.

If the man is unconscious it may be necessary for another crew member to go into the water to secure a rope around him. That person *must* be wearing a lifejacket and have a separate lifeline attached to the boat.

• Lifting out

To lift the man out of the water, attach one of the sail halyards to him and use the winch. Alternatively, you can clip the luff of a small sail (such as the storm jib) on to the guardrail; lower the bight of the sail into the water and float it under him. Then attach the halyard to the clew of the sail and winch him out of the water. If it can be done quickly it may be worth inflating the dinghy and getting him into that first.

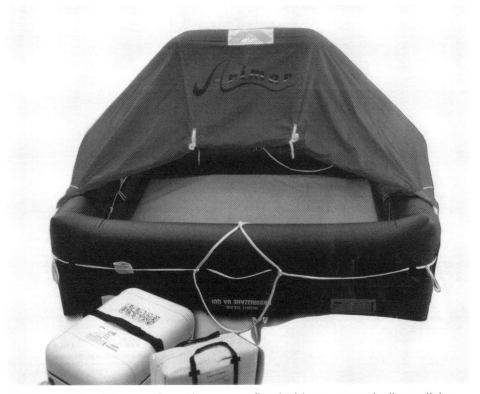

This type of liferaft has a self-erecting canopy fitted with an automatic distress light and retro-reflective foil.

Collision

In many emergencies it is difficult to establish a correct priority. Traditionally, the safety of the boat comes first and the safety of the crew second. If a boat has been in a collision, the first priority is normally to control the flooding. Once it has been established that the boat itself is in no further danger of sinking or catching fire, then any injuries to the crew can be treated.

To stop a flood, push blankets or sleeping bags into the hole from the inside and, if possible, drape a sail over the hole from the outside. It has been said that a frightened man with a bucket is the best way of emptying a boat full of water, however, in reality, the main bilge pump with high capacity should be used. The toilet pump may also be used, particularly if a length of tubing from the bilges is fed into the pan of the toilet. The hose from the engine cooling water system could possibly be disconnected and placed in the bilges. When the engine is run water will be sucked up through it and discharged overboard.

Fire

If a fire is discovered on board, the first thing to do is shout FIRE to alert everyone on board to the danger. Move everything inflammable out of the way and attempt to extinguish the fire.

A fire needs three things for it to take hold and spread:

- Fuel
- Oxygen
- Heat

Remove one or more of these elements and the fire will be eliminated.

Fuel Cut off the fuel source by turning off the gas and remove any combustible materials such as gas cylinders, fuel containers or pyrotechnics from the area near the fire.

Oxygen Starve the fire of oxygen by smothering it, using fire extinguishers or a fire blanket.

Heat Cool the fire by attacking the base of it with a fire extinguisher.

Fire extinguishers

Fire extinguishers are coded with a letter and a number denoting the category and size of fire for which they are suitable. Those approved to European standard will carry a BS EN3 certification mark.

Fire-fighting mediums contained in extinguishers include water (which should not be used on an oil or electrical fire), foam, powder and carbon dioxide. Sea water can also be used, especially for damping down an area.

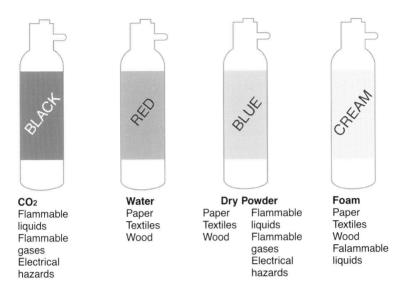

CO2	**Water**	**Dry Powder**		**Foam**
Flammable liquids	Paper	Paper	Flammable liquids	Paper
Flammable gases	Textiles	Textiles	Flammable gases	Textiles
Electrical hazards	Wood	Wood	Electrical hazards	Wood
				Falammable liquids

Types of fire extinguishers showing the colour codes for the contents and their uses.

Fire blanket

One of the most common sources of fire is a frying pan which has caught alight. If this happens, turn off the gas and smother the pan with the fire blanket or a heavy piece of damp cloth. Place the blanket over the fire away from you so as not to fan flames towards you. Never throw a burning pan overboard in case of spillage.

Action to be taken

If a fire breaks out and appears to be getting out of hand, inflate the dinghy and tow it astern; see that the liferaft is ready (but do not launch it until you abandon the boat); don lifejackets and standby to initiate distress procedures. Make sure no-one is trapped below.

Fire safety

- Keep the bilges clean
- Do not smoke in your bunk
- See that you are familiar with the fire-fighting equipment, its stowage and operation

Fuelling

When fuelling, follow the guidelines below:

- Stop the engine
- Turn off the cooker at the gas bottle and then at the cooker taps

- Extinguish naked flames and do not smoke
- Close hatches
- See that the tank does not overflow and mop up any spills immediately using detergent and water
- After fuelling see that the fuel cap is secure
- Ventilate the boat
- Use only approved containers for spare fuel and stow in a well-ventilated compartment.

Gas

When using gas cylinders on board, follow the guidelines below:

- See that all fittings are correctly installed and that there are no leaks.
- Stow gas cylinders in a container in the cockpit which drains overboard.
- When not in use, turn gas off from the cylinder, burn the gas out of the pipes and turn off at the cooker.
- Do not leave a lit cooker unattended.
- After replacing a cylinder check for leaks by smearing the joint between the valve and the bottle with soapy water. If bubbles appear there is a leak.

Accidents

Before leaving harbour the skipper should check whether anyone is likely to require special medical attention or is taking medication. Every crew member should be able to treat minor ailments and, in the event of a major accident, be able to make the patient as comfortable as possible so that injuries may be contained until help arrives.

Minor accidents

- *Small cuts*

Wash and cleanse with disinfectant and cover with a plaster or dressing.

- *Burns and scalds*

Immediately flood the area with cold water for at least 10 minutes, then cover with a smooth, clean, dry cloth.

- *Bruises*

Apply a cold compress.

- *Seasickness*

Give the patient something to do which requires concentration. If severe, send him below and tell him to lie down.

Headache
Give aspirin or another type of tablet recommended for headache.

Sunburn
Cool with calamine lotion and cover to prevent further burning.

Strains and sprains
Rest the affected limb.

Major accidents

Severe bleeding
Pinch the flesh together and raise the limb or press pads of material on to the wound.

Internal bleeding
Lie the patient down, keep him warm and try to get help.

Dislocations and fractures
Immobilise the limb in the most comfortable position until help arrives.

Shock

This accompanies all injuries.

Symptoms
The patient appears pale, his skin feels clammy, he may be perspiring, vomiting, thirsty or over-anxious. His pulse may be weak.

Treatment
Lay the patient down with the head low and turned to one side. Loosen his clothing. Keep him warm by covering him with a sail, blanket or sleeping bag. Reassure him. If the underlying injury is not apparent, try to find and treat it.

Concussion/compression

Any head injuries can become serious. After any bleeding has been dealt with the patient should be watched for drowsiness, dilated pupils, garbled speech and bleeding from the ears or nose (especially if he has been unconscious). Fluid in the brain cavity or a depressed bone may be compressing the brain and the patient can go into a coma. These cases should always be referred to a doctor as soon as possible.

Fig 17.1 The recovery or coma position.

Coma position

Any patient liable to vomit should be placed into the position shown in Fig 17.1 so that he does not choke (provided that there is no injury to prevent this).

Hypothermia

Anyone who is rescued from cold water and whose inner body core has cooled, should be treated for hypothermia. If this is not done he could quickly die.

Contents of a first aid kit

• • • • •

The first aid kit should be kept in a watertight box and the contents listed on the outside of the box. The following is a basic kit:

Roll of plaster	Calomine lotion
Individual plasters	Safety pins
Large triangular bandages	Disinfectant
Small bandages	Aspirin
Lint	Seasickness tablets
Cotton wool	Indigestion tablets
Scissors	Exposure bag
Tweezers	First aid book
Eye lotion and eye bath	

First aid has been dealt with here only briefly. During the winter months it is a good idea to attend a first aid course and learn how to administer it thoroughly.

Symptoms

Collapse, feeling cold, shivering, cramp, irritability, unnatural quietness, lack of co-ordination, loss of energy, forgetfulness, pallor and cold to the touch.

Treatment

When lifted out of the water he should be treated with care and kept in a horizontal position.

Prevent further heat loss by protecting him from the wind and weather. Get him below and wrap him in a sleeping bag or several blankets. If an exposure blanket (a plastic sheet with a reflective surface) or a large plastic bag is available, this can be put round him to contain body heat. Unless medical advice is available rewarming should be slow *without* the use of hot water bottles. *No alcohol must be given.* Placing the patient near a warm engine will help.

Resuscitation

When breathing has stopped it is necessary to start resuscitation. Unless this is done within four minutes, brain damage may occur.

Expired air resuscitation

1 Lie the patient on his back.
2 Clear his mouth of obstructions and check whether he has swallowed his tongue (but do not waste time).
3 Tilt his head back and lift his jaw as shown in Fig 17.2. This lifts the tongue away from the back of the throat and creates an open airway.
4 Pinch his nose and blow firmly into his mouth or close his mouth with your thumb and blow gently but firmly into his nose. Whichever method is used see that a good seal is made. His chest should rise, if it does not, check for obstructions.
5 Turn your head away, wait for his chest to fall, take a breath and repeat. Initially, give 4 to 6 quick breaths and then one every 5 seconds.
6 Continue until he is breathing normally or until there is no hope of recovery.
7 If normal breathing is resumed watch him carefully to see that his breathing does not fail again.

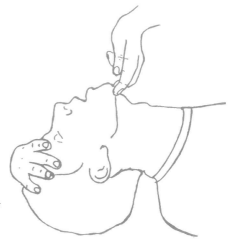

Fig 17.2 The correct position of the head for mouth-to-mouth resuscitation.

For small children and babies more rapid breathing is needed. Be careful not to blow too hard as the lungs may be damaged. If a person's heart has stopped beating, closed chest cardiac massage should be applied. This needs to be applied by an experienced first aider if it is to be successful.

Anyone who has suffered a hit on the head and become unconscious, has had severe hypothermia, or has recovered from an apparent drowning should be referred to a doctor as soon as possible.

Distress

All crew members must know the distress procedures and should acquaint themselves with the operation of flares and the signalling lamp (if available). A distress signal is only used when there is grave and imminent danger to the boat or crew. The distress signals are listed fully in Annexe IV of the International Regulations for Preventing Collisions at Sea.

Those suitable for a small boat are:

1 Continuous sounding of the fog horn.
2 The morse letters S O S by light or sound.
3 The word MAYDAY on the radio telephone.
4 International Code Flags N over C.
5 A square shape above or below a round shape.
6 A red rocket parachute flare or red hand flare.
7 An orange smoke signal by day.
8 Outstretched arms slowly and repeatedly raised and lowered.
9 Flames on the boat.
10 An explosive device (such as a gun) fired at intervals of one minute.

Pyrotechnics

Red flares

A red handflare (pinpoint flare) is used when you are within sight of land or another boat, or to pinpoint your position when rescuers are within visible range. It burns for 1 minute. Do not point it into the wind or you will be covered with sparks and smoke. Do not look directly at it.

A parachute rocket flare is used to raise the alarm when you are out of sight of land. It projects a very bright red parachute-suspended flare to a height of 300 metres which burns for 40 seconds. A rocket turns towards the wind and so should be fired vertically or, in strong winds, 15 degrees downwind. If there is low cloud it should be fired 45 degrees downwind so that the flare ignites below the cloud base.

Orange smokeflare

This is a daytime distress signal which produces a dense cloud of orange smoke easily seen from the air. In strong winds, however, the smoke blows along the sea surface and may not be visible from the shore or other boats. Handsmokes burn for 50 seconds and are used when rescuers are within visible range. Buoyant smokes, which consist of a canister with a ring pull, can be thrown into the water and burn for 3 minutes.

White handflare

This is not used for distress but to warn other boats of your position. It burns for 50 seconds. Do not look directly at it. White parachute flares are also available and are generally used for demonstration purposes. They are very useful to illuminate the area in a man overboard situation.

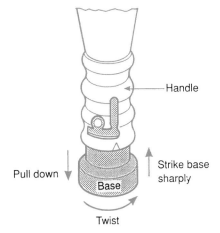

Fig 17.3 Firing a hand flare.

Firing flares

Firing a handflare (Fig 17.3):
1 Point downwind.
2 Hold the handle with one hand and pull the base of the handle with the other hand.
3 Twist the base of the handle to the right.
4 Strike the base of the handle with the palm of the hand or on a hard surface.
5 Hold the flare up and away from you.

Firing a parachute rocket flare (Fig 17.4):
1 Remove the top cap.
2 Remove the bottom cap.
3 Remove the safety pin.
4 The trigger will drop down.
5 Hold the signal ready to fire and squeeze the trigger.

These instructions are for Pains-Wessex Schermuly flares; other makes

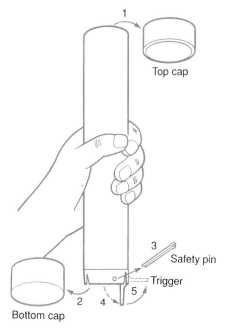

Fig 17.4 Firing a parachute rocket flare.

are operated differently. It is important that instructions are read and fully understood by every crew member so that action in an emergency will be prompt and correct.

Flare safety

1 Learn the purpose of the pyrotechnics and know how to use them.
2 Read and memorise the operating instructions on the flares and always follow these instructions *exactly.*
3 Stow in a secure, cool, dry place which is easily accessible and make sure that all crew members know where this is.
4 Always have at least the minimum required number and type of pyrotechnics on board and make sure that they are within their 'use by' date.
5 If a signal fails, hold it in the firing position for at least 30 seconds. Remove the caps and drop it into the sea.
6 Never point pyrotechnics at another person.
7 Out-of-date flares should be well weighted so that they will sink. They can then be disposed of in deep water.

Minimum recommended flare packs

In coastal waters up to 7 miles from land:
2 red parachute rockets
2 red handflares
2 handheld orange smokes

Offshore over 7 miles from land:
4 red parachute rockets
4 red handflares
2 buoyant orange smokes

For collision warning:
4 white handflares

VHF Radio telephone emergency procedure

The VHF (very high frequency) radio telephone is similar to a normal telephone, but usually has a switch which is depressed when speaking and released when listening. It is the quickest way to summon help. Its range is about 30 miles, dependent upon the height of the aerial.

Sending a distress (MAYDAY) call

This call is used when the vessel or a crew member is in grave and imminent danger.

1 Switch on the set and select Channel 16.
2 Listen to ensure that no other station is transmitting
3 Depress the press-to-speak switch and say MAYDAY three times.
4 Say the words 'THIS IS' and the BOAT'S NAME three times.
5 Repeat MAYDAY and the BOAT'S NAME once.
6 Give the boat's position either as latitude and longitude, or as a bearing *from* and distance off a known geographical point.
7 Give the nature of the distress and the assistance required.
8 Give the number of people on board.
9 End the message with the word 'OVER'.
10 Release the press-to-speak switch and wait. Repeat if there is no reply within 3 minutes.

● *Example*
MAYDAY MAYDAY MAYDAY
THIS IS YACHT JETTO YACHT JETTO YACHT JETTO
MAYDAY YACHT JETTO
MY POSITION IS ONE FIVE ZERO BEACHY HEAD LIGHT ONE POINT FIVE MILES
I AM SINKING AND NEED IMMEDIATE ASSISTANCE
I HAVE FOUR PERSONS ON BOARD
OVER

Sending an URGENCY (PAN PAN) call

This is used for a very urgent message concerning the safety of a person or the safety of the vessel. It is not yet a distress situation but may become so.

1 Switch on the set and select Channel 16.
2 Listen to ensure that no other station is transmitting.
3 Depress the press-to-speak switch and say PAN PAN three times.
4 Call anyone listening by saying the words ALL STATIONS three times.
5 Give the BOAT'S NAME three times.
6 Give the boat's position.
7 Give the reason for the call and the help needed.
8 End the message with the word 'OVER'.
9 Release the press-to-speak switch and wait for a reply.

- *Example*

PAN PAN PAN PAN PAN PAN
ALL STATIONS ALL STATIONS ALL STATIONS
THIS IS YACHT JETTO YACHT JETTO YACHT JETTO
MY POSITION IS TWO SEVEN ZERO FROM NEEDLES LIGHTHOUSE SIX
   MILES
MY ENGINE HAS FAILED I AM DRIFTING AND NEED A TOW URGENTLY
OVER

Medical assistance

If you have a sick crew member on board and are not sure of the diagnosis, medical advice can be obtained using the VHF radio telephone by including the word 'MEDICO' after the words 'PAN PAN'. The call is sent in exactly the same way as for a normal urgency call but is usually addressed to the nearest coast radio station instead of to all stations. After initial contact has been made on Channel 16 you may be asked to change to a less busy working channel if there is to be a lengthy conversation with a doctor.

Question Papers

Question Paper One

1.1 Fill in on the diagram:

    a.   Bow
    b.   Stern
    c.   Port side
    d.   Starboard side

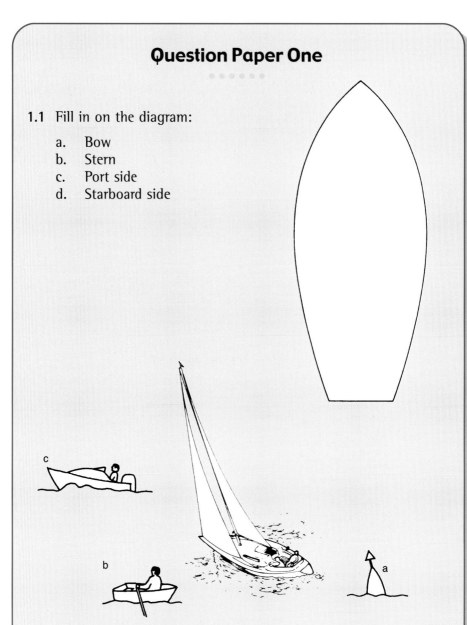

1.2 Study the diagram and answer the following questions. In relation to the boat, what position are:

    a.   The buoy
    b.   The rowing boat
    c.   The power boat

1.3 In the diagram the boat is approaching a buoy. How would you tell the skipper that you wish him to pass the buoy so that it is on the port side of the boat?

1.4 Fill in the following names on the diagrams:

a. Fore hatch
b. Main hatch
c. Cockpit
d. Mast
e. Boom
f. Pulpit
g. Pushpit
h. Guardrail
i. Stanchion
j. Keel
k. Rudder
l. Tiller

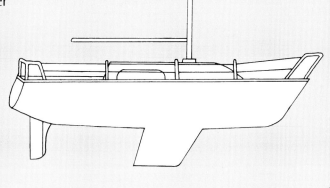

1.5 Name the parts of the sail (a–f).

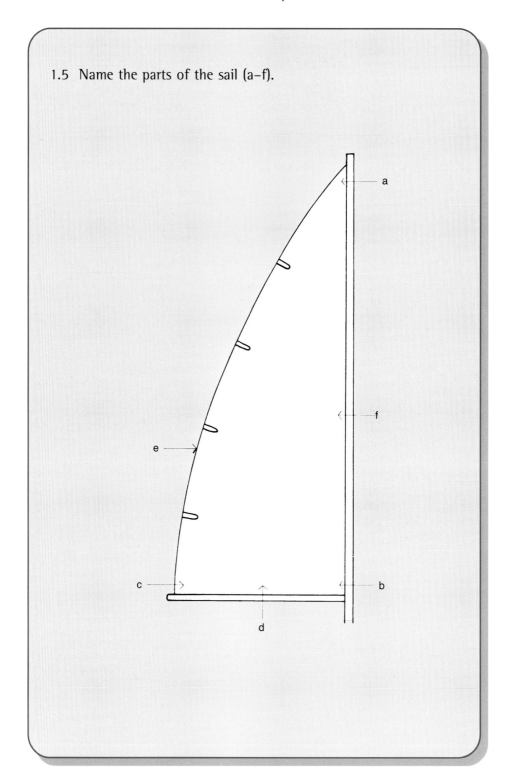

Question Paper Two

● ● ● ● ● ●

2.1 Fill in which point of sailing the boats are on and which tack.

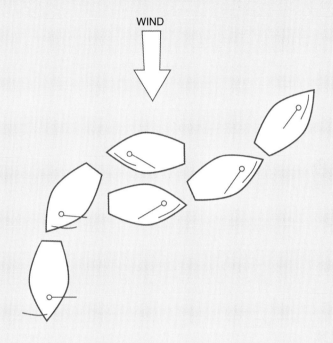

2.2 i What are the lines a, b, c and d called?
  ii What is their purpose?

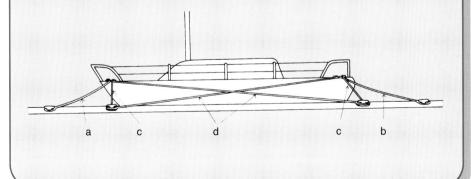

2.3 What are the parts of the anchor called?

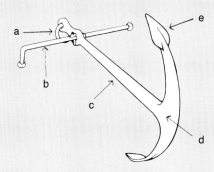

2.4 Show the position of the sails and the rudder when the boat is hove-to.

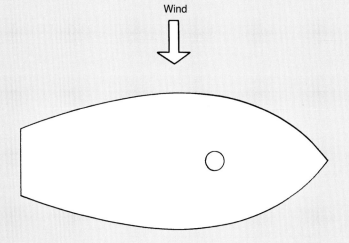

2.5 Why has the boat in the diagram laid a second anchor? The tidal stream is weak in the anchorage but a gale has been forecast.

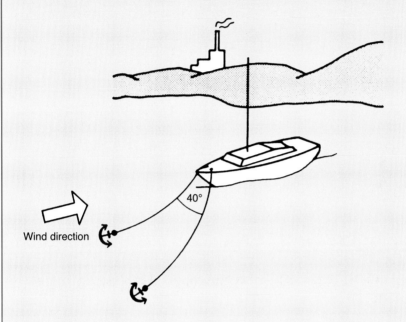

Wind direction

40°

Question Paper Three

3.1 What are the parts of the rope called?

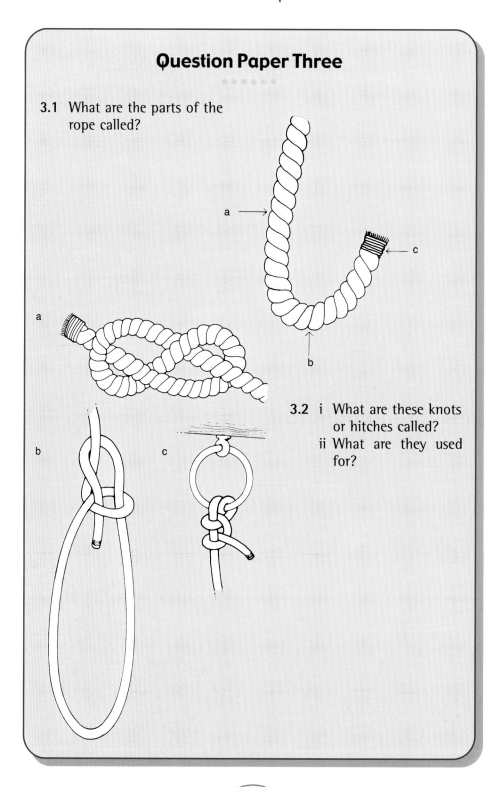

3.2 i What are these knots or hitches called?
ii What are they used for?

3.3 The boat in the diagram is carrying a full mainsail and a large genoa. A gale has been forecast. If she stays on the same course and the wind increases to force 8, what sails would you expect her to carry?

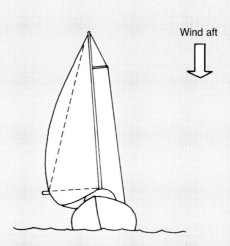

Wind aft

3.4 The boat in the diagram takes a compass bearing of the lighthouse and the radio mast when they are in transit which gives 356°C. The true bearing on the chart is 358°T. Variation is 6°W. What is the deviation?

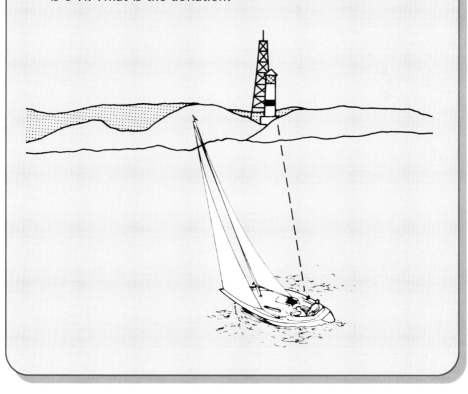

3.5 The diagram shows a hand-bearing compass being used to take a bearing. What corrections should be made to that bearing before it can be plotted on the chart?

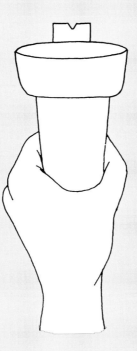

Question Paper Four

· · · · · · ·

4.1 Draw arrows to show the conventional direction of buoyage around the British Isles.

4.2 The boat is approaching a cardinal mark. Which side should she leave it?

4.3 The boat in the diagram has just anchored. How can she tell whether her anchor is dragging?

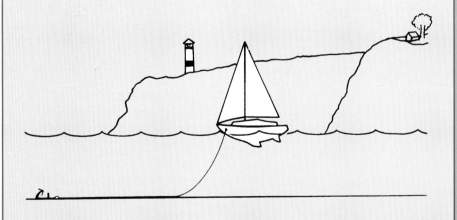

4.4 How can the boat use shore objects to enter the harbour safely?

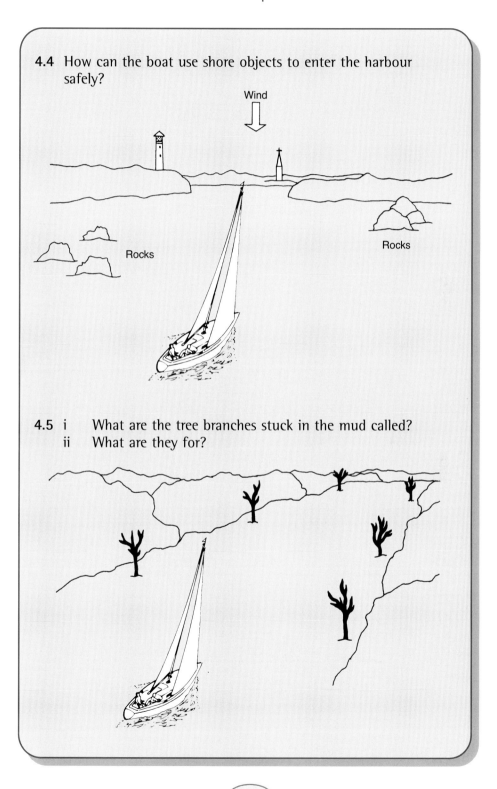

4.5 i What are the tree branches stuck in the mud called?
ii What are they for?

Question Paper Five

● ● ● ● ● ●

5.1 How can the power boat tell whether she is on a collision course with the sailing boat?

5.2 Who has right of way?

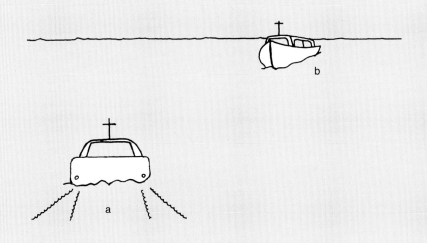

5.3 The sailing boat is overtaking the power boat. Who has right of way?

5.4 Why is the patient's head placed in this position before commencing expired air resuscitation?

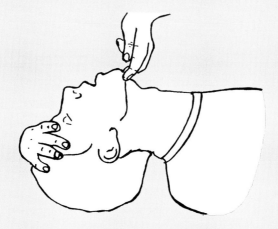

5.5 Yacht *Mermain* is holed and sinking rapidly. Her position is five miles from Land's End. The bearing of Land's End from the yacht is 060°T. There are six people on board. Write out the message she will send on the VHF radio telephone.

Answers to Question Papers

Question Paper One

1.1

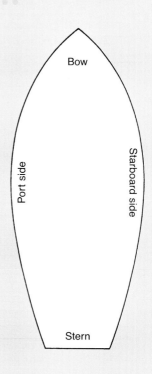

1.2 a. Astern.
     b. Abeam to port.
     c. Ahead.

1.3 Leave the buoy to port.

1.4

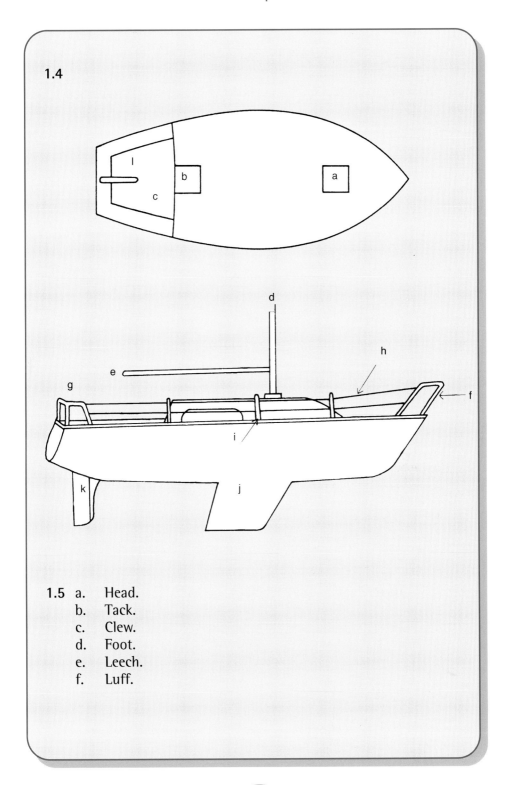

1.5 a. Head.
b. Tack.
c. Clew.
d. Foot.
e. Leech.
f. Luff.

Question Paper Two

••••••

2.1

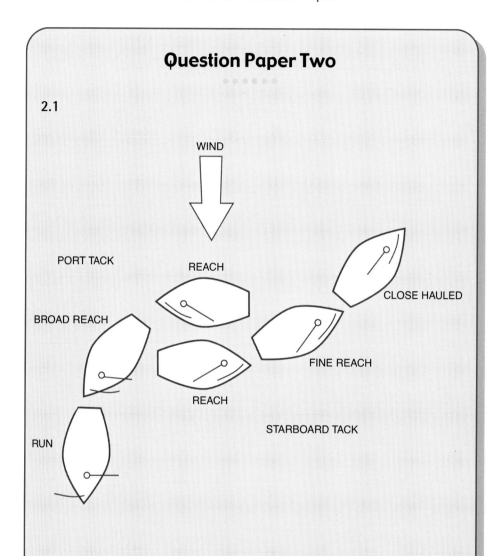

2.2 i   a. Bow line.   b. Stern line.   c. Breast lines.   d. Springs.

     ii   The bow and stern lines hold the boat's bows and stern in.
          The breast lines keep the boat alongside.
          The springs stop the boat moving fore and aft.

2.3 a. Ring.   b. Stock.   c. Shank.   d. Crown.   e. Fluke.

2.4

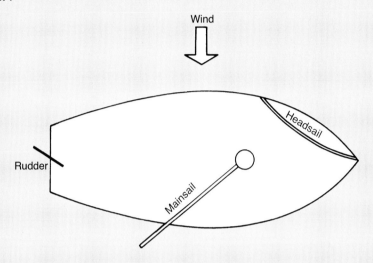

2.5 A second anchor has been laid to stop the boat yawing.

Question Paper Three

3.1 a. Standing part.
    b. Bight.
    c. End.

3.2 i   a. A stopper knot or figure of eight.
       b. A bowline.
       c. A round turn and two half hitches.
   ii   a. To stop the end of a sheet pulling through a block.
       b. To put a temporary eye in a rope.
       c. For securing a mooring line to a ring.

3.3 She would probably be running before the wind with a storm jib only.

3.4 Deviation 8°E.

3.5 Variation. If the hand-bearing compass is held well away from magnetic influences there should be no deviation.

Question Paper Four

4.1

4.2 To starboard.

4.3 By taking bearings of shore objects at regular intervals.

4.4 She can use clearing bearings from the lighthouse and the church to stay in safe water away from the rocks.

4.5 i   Withies.
     ii   They mark the safe channel.

Question Paper Five

● ● ● ● ● ●

5.1 By taking a compass bearing at regular intervals. If the bearing does not alter the boat is on a collision course.

5.2 b (a should go astern of b).

5.3 The power boat.

5.4 To create a clear airway.

5.5 MAYDAY MAYDAY MAYDAY
THIS IS YACHT MERMAIN YACHT MERMAIN YACHT MERMAIN
MAYDAY YACHT MERMAIN
MY POSITION IS TWO FOUR ZERO LANDS END FIVE MILES
I AM SINKING AND REQUIRE IMMEDIATE ASSISTANCE
I HAVE SIX PERSONS ON BOARD
OVER

Appendix I

Royal Yachting Association
Competent Crew Practical Course Syllabus

Aim: To introduce the complete beginner to cruising and to teach personal safety, seamanship and helmsmanship to the level required to be a useful member of the crew of a cruising yacht.

1 **Knowledge of sea terms and parts of a boat, her rigging and sails**
   Sufficient knowledge to understand orders given concerning the sailing and day-to-day running of the boat.
2 **Sail handling**
   Bending on, setting, reefing and handling of sails. Use of sheets and halyards and their associated winches.
3 **Ropework**
   Handling ropes, including coiling, stowing, securing to cleats and single and double bollards. Handling warps. Ability to tie the following knots and to know their correct use: figure of eight, clove hitch, rolling hitch, bowline, round turn and two half hitches, single and double sheet bend, reef knot.
4 **Fire precautions and fighting**
   Awareness of the hazards of fire, the precautions necessary to prevent fire and the action to be taken in event of fire.
5 **Personal safety equipment**
   Understands and complies with rules for the wearing of safety harnesses, lifejackets and personal buoyancy aids.
6 **Man overboard**
   Understands action to be taken to recover a man overboard.
7 **Distress signals**
   Can operate distress flares and knows on what occasions distress flares should be used.
8 **Manners and customs**
   Understands the ordinary practice of seamen and yachtsmen with regard to: use of burgees and ensigns, prevention of unnecessary noise or disturbance in harbour, including courtesies to other craft berthed alongside.
9 **Rules of the road**
   Is able to keep an efficient lookout at sea.

10 **Dinghies**
Understands and complies with the loading rules. Is able to handle a dinghy under oars.

11 **Meteorology**
Awareness of forecasting services and knowledge of the Beaufort scale.

12 **Seasickness**
Working efficiency unaffected/partially affected/severely affected by seasickness.

13 **Helmsmanship and sailing**
Understands the theory of sailing and can steer and trim sails on all points of sailing. Can steer a compass course, under sail and power.

Appendix II

Safety List for a Small Boat

The amount and type of safety equipment carried depends upon the size and type of boat and its cruising area. Recommended lists for craft under 13.7 metres can be found in RYA booklet *Cruising Yacht Safety*. Racing boats may be subject to special rules.

Any boat of 13.7 metres and over must conform to the standards laid down in the Merchant Shipping Rules; below this size safety equipment is not compulsory but is strongly recommended. A general guide to the basic equipment which should be carried on board is given below:

1 An approved liferaft of a size suitable to accommodate all persons on board, carried where it can be quickly launched.
2 A half-inflated dinghy. This can be used instead of a liferaft but is a poor alternative in anything but sheltered waters near the shore.
3 Two lifebuoys, one with a light and a drogue and one with 30 metres of floating line (or a rescue quoit with floating line attached).
4 A dan buoy with a light and a drogue.
5 A lifejacket for every crew member.
6 A safety harness for every crew member.
7 Suitable safety harness anchorages.
8 Strong and adequate guardrails and lifelines.
9 An approved pack of flares with at least two red parachute rockets.
10 A first aid box.
11 A waterproof torch.
12 A method of securing and releasing the main hatch and hatch boards from either side.
13 The name of the boat on the spray dodgers and on a piece of canvas ready to display if necessary. Letters to be at least 22cm in height.
14 A method of securing any heavy gear (such as batteries) so that they will not damage the boat in heavy weather.
15 Adequate and efficient navigation lights.
16 Two anchors of sufficient size with enough warp and/or chain for the maximum expected depth.
17 One fixed and one portable bilge pump.
18 A radar reflector.
19 Sufficient up-to-date charts and pilot books.

20 A steering compass.
21 A hand-bearing compass.
22 A radio receiver for weather reports.
23 A radio direction finder.
24 A radio telephone (VHF).
25 A distance log.
26 A tow line.
27 A tool kit which includes a hacksaw and bolt cutters.
28 A separate engine battery which can be isolated from the lighting battery.
29 At least two fire extinguishers of an approved type.
30 A fire blanket.
31 A bag of sand for oil fires.
32 Two strong buckets with lanyards.

Appendix III

Glossary

Aback A sail is aback when the wind strikes it on what would normally be its lee side.

Abaft the beam The sector on both sides of a boat from abeam to astern.

Abeam The direction at right angles to the fore-and-aft line.

Abate The true wind abates or moderates when it blows less strongly than before.

Adrift Not attached to the sea-bed.

Afloat Floating; at sea.

Aft Near or towards the stern.

Ahead The direction of an object beyond the stem of a boat.

Ahoy Shout this to attract attention of another vessel.

Alee To leeward.

Almanac An annual publication containing information on, for example, buoyage, tides, signals, glossaries, and positions of heavenly bodies.

Aloft Above deck.

Amidships The centre part of the boat.

Anchor buoy Buoy or float secured by a tripping line to the crown of the anchor.

Anchor cable Chain or rope connection between a boat and her anchor.

Anchor light An all round white light usually shackled to the forestay of a boat and hoisted to a suitable height by the jib halyard.

Anchor locker A locker for the anchor and anchor chain.

Anchor roller A roller over which the anchor cable is passed when at anchor.

Anchor watch Watch kept when a boat is at anchor to check whether the anchor is dragging.

Anchor well See *anchor locker*.

Answer the helm A boat answers the helm when she alters course in response to the helmsman's deflection of the rudder.

Apparent wind The wind felt by the crew in a boat that is moving over the ground.

Ashore On the land; or aground.

Astern Direction beyond the stern; or a movement through the water in that direction.

Athwartships At right angles to the centreline of the boat inside the boat.

Autopilot Equipment that allows the boat to follow automatically a compass course or a course relative to wind direction.

Auxiliary A term for a sailing boat that has auxiliary power, i.e. an engine.

Avast Order to stop an activity.

Awash Level with the surface of the water which just washes over an object.

Babystay An inner forestay.

Back To back a sail: it is sheeted or held to windward so that the wind strikes it on the side which is normally to leeward. Of wind: it backs when it shifts to blow from a direction that is further anticlockwise.

Back splice The end of a rope that has been finished by unlaying the strands, making a crown knot and tucking the strands back down the rope.

Backstay A stay which supports the mast from aft.

Backwind Airflow that is deflected on to the lee side of a sail, such as a jib backwinding the mainsail.

Bail To remove water from the bilges or cockpit.

Bailer A utensil used to bail water out of a boat.

Ball A black signal shape normally displayed by day when a boat is at anchor.

Ballast Additional weight placed low in the hull to improve stability.

Bar A shoal close by a river mouth or harbour entrance; a measure of barometric pressure usually noted as 1000 millibars.

Bare poles No sails are set and the boat is driven by the force of the wind on the spars and rigging.

Barnacle A marine crustacean that attaches itself to the bottom of a boat.

Batten A flexible strip of wood or plastic used to stiffen the leech of a sail.

Batten pocket A pocket on the leech of a sail to contain a batten.

Beach To run a boat ashore deliberately.

Beacon A mark erected on land or on the bottom in shallow waters to guide or warn shipping.

Beam The breadth of a boat.

Beam reach A point of sailing with the wind roughly at right angles to the fore-and-aft line.

Bear The direction of an object from an observer.

Bear away To put the helm to windward so that the boat alters course to leeward away from the wind.

Bearing The direction of an object from an observer given as an angle from a line of reference (true north or magnetic north).

Bearings (3-figure notation) Bearings and courses are given in a 3-figure notation, that is: 180°C or 180°T depending on whether it is a Compass or True bearing.

Beating Sailing towards an objective to windward following a zigzag course on alternate tacks.

Beaufort scale A scale for measurement of the force of the wind.

Belay To make fast a line round a cleat or bollard.

Bell In restricted visibility a bell is rung to indicate that a boat is at anchor or aground.

Below deck Beneath the deck.

Bend To connect two ropes with a knot; to prepare a sail for hoisting; a type of knot.

Berth A place where a boat can lie for a period; a sleeping place on a boat (see *bunk*); to give an obstruction a wide berth by keeping well clear.

Bight A loop or curve in a rope or line.

Bilge The rounded part of a boat where the bottom curves upwards towards the sides.

Bilges The lowest part inside the hull below the cabin sole where bilge water collects.

Bilge keel One of two keels fitted on either side of a boat's hull to resist rolling and provide lateral resistance.

Binnacle Strong housing to protect the steering compass.

Blanket To take the wind from another boat's sails.

Blast (foghorn) A sound signal – a short blast lasts 1 second, a prolonged blast 4 to 6 seconds.

Block A pulley made of wood, metal or plastic.

Boathook A pole, generally of wood or light alloy, with a hook at one end, used for picking up moorings and buoys.

Bollard Strong fitting, firmly bolted to the deck, to which mooring lines are made fast. Large bollards are on quays, piers and pontoons.

Bolt rope Rope sewn to one or more edges of a sail either to reinforce the sides or so that the sail can be fed into a grooved spar.

Boom Spar that supports the foot of the sail.

Boom out On a run to thrust the genoa out to windward with a whisker pole so that it fills with wind.

Boot top A narrow stripe just above the waterline between the bottom and side of the hull. Usually of contrasting colour.

Bottlescrew A rigging screw to tension the standing rigging or guardrails.

Bow The forward part of a boat. A direction 45° either side of right ahead.

Bowline A knot tied in the end of a line to make a loop that will neither slip nor jam.

Breakwater A structure built to protect a harbour or beach from the force of the sea.

Breast rope A mooring line that runs at right angles to the centreline; one runs from the bow, another from the stern to the shore or a boat alongside.

Broach With heavy following seas the boat can slew round uncontrollably, heeling dangerously.

Breather A pipe fitted to a water or fuel tank which allows air to escape.

Broad reach The point of sailing between a beam reach and a run.

Broken out The anchor, when pulled out of the seabed by heaving on the cable, is broken out.

Bulkhead A vertical partition below decks.

Bunk A built-in sleeping place.

Buoy A floating object used to indicate the position of a channel, wreck, danger, etc., or the position of an object on the seabed.

Buoyancy aid A life-preserver to help a person float if he falls in; less effective than a lifejacket.

Burgee A triangular flag worn at the masthead.

Cabin The sheltered area in which the crew live and sleep.

Cable Chain or rope that is made fast to the anchor. A measure of distance equivalent to one tenth of a nautical mile.

Capsize The boat overturns.

Cast off To let go a rope or line.

Cavita line A decorative line of contrasting colour on the hull of the boat, near the rubbing strake.

Centreboard A board lowered through a slot in the keel to reduce leeway by providing lateral resistance.

Chafe Damage or wear resulting from friction.

Chain locker See *anchor locker*.

Chainplate A fitting which is bolted to the hull, to which the shrouds are attached.

Chandler A shop which sells nautical gear.

Channel A waterway through shoals, rivers or harbours.

Chart Printed map giving many details about the area covered by water and details about the adjacent land.

Chart datum Reference level on charts and for use in tidal predictions.

Clear To disentangle a line; to avoid a danger or obstruction; improved weather.

Cleat A fitting with two horns round which a rope is secured.

Clevis pin A locking pin with an eye at one end through which a split ring is fitted to prevent accidental withdrawal.

Clew The after lower corner of a sail to which the sheets are fitted.

Clew outhaul The line which tensions the foot of the mainsail.

Close hauled The point of sailing when the boat is as close to the wind as she can lie with advantage in working to windward.

Coachroof The part of the cabin that is raised above the deck to provide height in the cabin.

Coaming Vertical structure surrounding a hatch or cockpit to prevent water entering.

Coast radio station A radio station for communication between ships at sea and the public telephone network.

Coastguard The organisation responsible for search and rescue operations in UK waters.

Cocked hat In navigation the triangle formed when three position lines fail to meet at a single point.

Cockpit A space lower than deck level in which the crew can sit or stand.

Collision course The course of a boat which, if maintained relative to that of another, would result in a collision.

Compass rose A circle printed on a chart representing the true compass and graduated clockwise from 0° to 360°.

Cone A signal shape displayed either point upwards or point downwards.

Counter Above the waterline where the stern extends beyond the rudder post forming a broad afterdeck abaft the cockpit.

Course The direction in which the boat is being, or is to be, steered.

Courtesy ensign The national flag of the country being visited by a foreign boat; it should be flown from the starboard spreader.

CQR anchor A patented anchor with good holding power.

Cringle A rope loop, usually with a metal thimble, worked in the edge of a sail.

Crutch see Rowlock. Also a support for the boom when the mainsail is lowered.

Dan buoy A temporary mark to indicate a position, say, of a man overboard. A flag flies from a spar passing through a float and weighted at the bottom.

Deck log A book in which all matters concerning navigation are entered or logged.

Depth sounder See *Echo sounder*.

Deviation The deflection of the needle of a magnetic compass caused by the proximity of ferrous metals, electrical circuits or electronic equipment.

Diaphone A fog signal low pitched and powerful with a grunt at the end.

Dip the ensign To lower the ensign briefly as a salute. It is not rehoisted until the vessel saluted has dipped and rehoisted hers in acknowledgement.

Direction finder A radio receiver with a directional aerial with which the bearing of a radio beacon can be found.

Displacement The weight of a boat defined as the weight of water displaced by that boat.

Distance made good The distance covered over the ground having made allowance for tidal stream and leeway.

Dividers Navigational instrument for measuring distances on charts.

Dodger Screen fitted to give the crew protection from wind and spray.

Dolphin A mooring post or group of piles.

Double up To put out extra mooring lines when a storm is expected.

Douse To lower a sail or extinguish a light quickly.

Downhaul A rope or line with which a spar or sail is pulled down.

Downwind Direction to leeward.

Downstream The direction towards which the stream flows.

Drag The anchor drags when it fails to hold and slides over the sea-bed.

Draught The vertical distance from the lowest part of the keel to the waterline.

Dredger A vessel designed for dredging a channel.

Dress ship On special occasions ships in harbour or at anchor dress overall with International Code flags from the stem to the mast head and down to the stern.

Drift To be carried by the tidal stream. The distance that a boat is carried by the tidal stream in a given time.

Drifter A fishing vessel that lies to her nets.

Drop astern To fall astern of another boat.

Drop keel A keel that can be drawn up into the hull.

Ease out To slacken a rope gradually.

Ebb The period when the tidal level is falling.

Echo sounder An electronic depth-finding instrument.

Ensign The national flag worn at or near the stern of a boat to indicate her nationality.

EPIRB An Emergency Position Indicating Radio Beacon that transmits a distinctive signal on a distress frequency.

Even keel A boat floating so that her mast is more or less vertically upright.

Eye A loop or eye splice. The eyes of a boat: right forward.

Eyelet A small hole in a sail with a metal grommet through which lacing is passed.

Eye splice A permanent eye spliced in the end of a rope or wire rope.

Fair Advantageous or favourable, as of wind or tide.

Fairlead The lead through which a working line is passed in order to alter the direction of pull.

Fairway The main channel in a body of water such as an estuary or river.

Fender Any device hung outboard to absorb the shock when coming alongside and to protect the hull when moored alongside.

Fetch The distance travelled by the wind when crossing open water: the height of the waves is proportional to the fetch and strength of the wind.

Fin keel A short keel bolted to the hull.

Fix The position of a boat as plotted on the chart from position lines obtained by compass bearings, direction finder, echo sounder, etc.

Flake down Rope laid down on deck in a figure of eight pattern so that it will run out easily.

Flashing A light used as an aid to navigation that flashes repeatedly at regular intervals where the dark period exceeds the light period.

Flood The period when the tidal level is rising.

Fluke The shovel-shaped part of an anchor that digs into the ground.

Flying out A sail is flying out in a breeze when it has no tension in the sheets.

Focsle The part of the accommodation below the foredeck and forward of the mast.

Fog Visibility reduced to less than 1000 metres (approx. 0.5 nautical miles).

Foghorn A horn with which fog signals are made.

Following sea Seas that are moving in the same direction as the boat is heading.

Foot The lower edge of a sail.

Fore-and-aft Parallel to the line between the stem and the stern.

Foredeck The part of the deck that is forward of the mast and coachroof.

Forefoot The area below the water where the stem joins the keel.

Forehatch A hatch forward, usually in the foredeck.

Forepeak The most forward compartment in the bows of the boat.

Foresail The headsail set on the forestay.

Forestay The stay from high on the mast to the stemhead providing fore-and-aft support for the mast.

Foul The opposite of clear; adverse (wind or tide); unsuitable.

Foul anchor An anchor whose flukes are caught on an obstruction on the sea-bed or tangled with the cable.

Frap Tie halyards to keep them off the mast to stop them rattling noisily in the wind when in harbour.

Freeboard The vertical distance between the waterline and the top of the deck.

Free wind The wind when it blows from a direction abaft the beam.

Front (air mass) Boundary between air masses at different temperatures.

Full and by Close-hauled with all sails full and drawing; not pinching.

Full rudder The maximum angle to which the rudder can be turned.

Furling Rolling up or gathering and lashing a lowered sail using sail ties or shockcord to prevent it from blowing about.

Gale In the Beaufort scale, wind force 8, 34 to 40 knots. Severe gale, force 9, is 41 to 47 knots.

Galley An area where food is prepared and cooked.

Gelcoat The outer unreinforced layer of resin in a Glass Reinforced Plastic (GRP) hull.

Genoa A large overlapping headsail set in light to fresh winds.

Ghoster A light full headsail set in light breezes.

Give-way vessel The vessel whose duty it is to keep clear of another; she should take early and substantial action to avoid a collision.

Go about To change from one tack to another by luffing and turning the bows through the wind.

Gong A fog signal sounded in conjunction with a bell in a vessel over 100m in length when at anchor or aground.

Gooseneck Fitting which attaches the boom to the mast.

Goosewing To fly the headsail on the opposite side to the mainsail (using a spinnaker pole or whisker pole perhaps) when running.

Grab rail Rails fitted above and below decks to hold on to when the boat heels.

Ground To run aground or touch the bottom either accidentally or deliberately.

Ground tackle A general term for the anchors, cables and all the gear required when anchoring.

Groyne See *Breakwater*.

GRP Glass Reinforced Plastic.

Guardrail Safety line fitted round the boat to prevent the crew from falling overboard.

Gunwale The upper edge of the side of a boat.

Guy A line attached to the end of a spar to keep it in position.

Gybe To change from one tack to another by turning the stern through the wind.

Gybe-oh The warning given when the helm is put across to gybe.

Hail To shout loudly to crew in another boat.

Half hitch A simple knot.

Halyard A line or rope with which a sail, spar or flag is hoisted up a mast.

Hand-bearing compass Portable magnetic compass with which visual bearings are taken.

Handrail A wooden or metal rail on the coachroof or below deck which can be grasped to steady a person.

Hanks Fittings made of metal or nylon by which the luff of a staysail is held to a stay.

Hard Hard ground where boats can be launched.

Hard and fast Said of a boat that has run aground and is unable to get off immediately.

Harden in To haul in the sheets to bring the sail closer to the centreline; the opposite of *ease out*.

Hatch An opening in the deck that allows access to the accommodation.

Haul in To pull in.

Hawse pipe A hole in the bow of a vessel through which the anchor cable passes.

Haze Visibility reduced to between 1,000 and 2,000 metres (0.5 to 1 nautical mile) by dry particles in suspension in the air.

Head The bow or forward part of the boat. The upper corner of a triangular sail.

Head line The mooring line or rope leading forward from the bows.

Head to wind To point the stem of the boat into the wind.

Heading The direction in which the boat's head is pointing, her course.

Headland A fairly high and steep part of the land that projects into the sea.

Heads The lavatory on a boat.

Headsail Any sail set forward of the mast or of the foremast if there is more than one mast.

Headway Movement through the water stem first.

Heat seal To fuse the ends of the strands of a man-made fibre rope by heating.

Heaving line A light line coiled ready for throwing; sometimes the end is weighted.

Heaving-to A boat heaves-to when she goes about leaving the headsail sheeted on the original side so it is backed. Ideal manoeuvre for reefing in heavy weather.

Heel To lean over to one side.

Height of tide The vertical distance at any instant between sea level and chart datum.

Helmsman The member of the crew who steers the boat.

Hitch A type of knot.

Hoist To raise an object vertically with a halyard.

Holding ground The composition of the sea-bed that determines whether the anchor will hold well or not.

Hull The body of a boat excluding masts, rigging and rudder.

Hull down Said of a distant vessel when only the mast, sails and/or superstructure is visible above the horizon.

Hurricane In the Beaufort scale, wind of force 12, 64 knots or above.

Hydrofoil A boat with hydrofoils that lift the wetted surface of her hull clear of the water at speed.

Hydrography The science of surveying the waters of the earth and adjacent land areas and publishing the results in charts, pilots, etc.

IALA The International Association of Lighthouse Authorities which is responsible for the international buoyage system.

Impeller Screw-like device which is rotated by water flowing past: used for measuring boat speed and distance travelled through the water.

In irons Said of a boat that stops head to wind when going about.

Inflatable dinghy A dinghy made of synthetic rubber filled with air; can be deflated for stowage on board.

Inshore Near to or towards or in the direction of the shore.

Isobar On a synoptic chart, a line joining points of equal pressure.

Isophase A light where the duration of light and dark are equal.

Jackstay A wire secured between two points.

Jam cleat (self-jamming) A cleat with one horn shorter than the other designed so that a rope can be secured with a single turn.

Jib Triangular headsail set on a stay forward of the mast.

Jury rig A temporary but effective device that replaces lost or damaged gear.

Kedge anchor A lightweight anchor used to move a boat or to anchor temporarily in fine weather.

Keel The main longitudinal beam on a boat between the stem and the stern.

Ketch A two-masted boat where the after (mizzen) mast is smaller and is stepped forward of the rudder stock.

kHz (kilohertz) A measurement of frequency of radio waves equivalent to 1,000 cycles per second.

Kicking strap Line or tackle to pull the boom down in order to keep it horizontal.

Kink A sharp twist in a rope or wire rope; can be avoided by coiling the rope properly.

Knot The unit of speed at sea; one nautical mile per hour; a series of loops in rope or line.

Landfall Land first sighted after a long voyage at sea.

Lanyard A short length of line used to secure an object such as a knife.

Lash down To secure firmly with rope or line.

Lay Strands twisted together to form a rope. To lay a mark is to sail directly to it without tacking.

Lead line A line marked with knots at regular intervals and attached to a heavy weight to determine the depth of water.

Lee The direction towards which the wind blows.

Leeboard A board or strip of canvas along the open side of a berth to prevent the occupant from falling out.

Lee helm The tendency of a boat to turn her bow to leeward.

Lee-oh The warning given when the helm is put across to go about.

Leech The trailing edge of a triangular or quadrilateral sail.

Lee shore A coastline towards which the onshore wind blows; the shore to leeward of a boat.

Leeward Downwind, away from the wind, the direction towards which the wind blows.

Leeward boat When two boats are on the same tack, the leeward boat is that which is to leeward of the other.

Leeway The angular difference between the water track and the boat's heading. The effect of wind moving the boat bodily to leeward.

Lifeline A wire or line attached at either end to a strong point and rigged along the deck as a handhold or for clipping on a safety harness.

Line Alternative name for small size rope or for a rope used for mooring a boat.

Line of soundings Numerous soundings taken at regular intervals.

List A permanent lean to one side or the other.

List of lights Official publication giving details of lights exhibited as aids to navigation.

Lively Said of a boat that responds rapidly to the seas.

LOA Length overall.

Loafer A lightweight sail used when reaching or running in light winds.

Lock A chamber in a navigation with gates at each end in which the water level can be raised or lowered.

Locker An enclosed stowage anywhere on board.

Locking turns A reversed turn on a cleat to make a rope more secure; not advisable for halyards which may need to be cast off quickly.

Log A device to measure a boat's speed or distance travelled through the water. See *Deck Log.*

Log reading The reading of distance travelled through the water usually taken every hour from the log and recorded in the deck log.

Look-out Visual watch; or the member of the crew responsible for keeping a visual watch.

Loom The glow from a light below the horizon usually seen as a reflection on the clouds.

Lop Short choppy seas.

Lose way A boat loses way when she slows down and stops in the water.

Lubber line The marker in the compass which is aligned with the fore-and-aft line of the boat against which the course can be read off on the compass card.

Luff The leading edge of a fore-and-aft sail.

Lull A temporary drop in wind speed.

Mainsail The principal sail.

Mainsheet traveller The athwartships slider to which the mainsheet tackle is made fast.

Make fast To secure a line or rope to a cleat, mooring ring, bollard, etc.

Make heavy weather Said of a yacht which rolls and pitches heavily, making slow and uncomfortable progress.

Make sail To hoist the sails and get under way.

Make water To leak but not by shipping water over the side.

Marina Artificial boat harbour usually consisting of pontoons.

Mark An object that marks a position.

Maroon An explosive signal used to summon the crew when a lifeboat is called out.

Mast The most important vertical spar without which no sail can be set.

Mast step Fitting into which the mast heel fits.

Masthead light A white light exhibited near the masthead by a power-driven vessel under way.

Masthead rig A boat with the forestay attached to the masthead.

Mayday The internationally recognised radio telephone distress signal.

Medico When included in an urgency call (Pan Pan) on the radio telephone, Medico indicates that medical advice is required.

MHWS (Mean High Water Springs) The average level of all high water heights at spring tides throughout the year: used as the datum level for heights of features on the chart.

Mist Visibility reduced to between 1,000 and 2,000 metres (0.5 to 1 nautical miles) due to the suspension of water particles in the air.

Mizzen mast The smaller aftermast of a ketch or yawl.

Mole A breakwater made of stone or concrete.

Monohull A boat with a single hull.

Mooring The ground tackle attached to a mooring buoy.

Mooring buoy A non-navigational buoy to which a boat can moor.

Mooring ring A ring on a mooring pile to which head and stern lines are secured.

Multihull A boat with more than one hull such as a catamaran or trimaran.

Nautical almanac Official publication giving positions of heavenly bodies and other information to enable a boat's position to be established.

Nautical mile Unit of distance at sea based on the length of one minute of latitude.

Navel pipe A pipe which passes through the deck to the anchor chain locker.

Navigation lights Lights exhibited by all vessels between sunset and sunrise.

Neap tide Tides where the range is least and the tidal streams run least strongly.

Near gale Wind of Beaufort force 7, 28 to 33 knots.

No-sail sector An area either side of the wind, in which a boat cannot sail.

Nominal range of a light Nominal range of a light is dependent on its intensity: it is the luminous range when the meteorological visibility is 10 nautical miles.

Not under command A vessel unable to manoeuvre such as one whose rudder has been damaged.

Notices to mariners Official notices issued weekly or at other times detailing corrections to charts and hydrographic publications.

Null The bearing of a radio beacon at which the signal tends to disappear when the aerial of a direction finder is rotated.

Occulting light A rhythmic light eclipsing at regular intervals so that the duration of light in each period is greater than the duration of darkness.

Offing The part of the sea that is visible from the shore. To keep an offing is to keep a safe distance from the shore.

Oilskins Waterproof clothing worn in foul weather.

On the bow A direction about 45° from right ahead on either side of the boat.

On the quarter A direction about 45° from right astern on either side of the boat.

Open When two leading marks are not in line they are said to be open.

Osmosis Water absorption through tiny pinholes in a GRP hull causing deterioration of the moulding.

Outhaul A line with which the mainsail clew is hauled out along the boom.

Overcanvassed A boat carrying too much sail for the weather conditions.

Overfalls Turbulent water where there is a sudden change in depth or where two tidal streams meet.

Overtaking light The white stern light; seen by an overtaking vessel when approaching from astern.

Painter The line at the bow of a dinghy.

Pan pan The internationally recognised radio telephone urgency signal which has priority over all other calls except Mayday.

Parallel rules Navigational instrument used in conjunction with the compass rose on a chart to transfer bearings and courses to plot a boat's position.

Pay off The boat's head pays off when it turns to leeward away from the wind.

Pay out To let out a line or rope gradually.

Period Of a light, the time that it takes a rhythmic light to complete one sequence.

Pile A stout timber, concrete or metal post driven vertically into a river or seabed.

Pilot An expert in local waters who assists vessels entering or leaving harbour. An official publication listing details of, for example, local coasts, dangers and harbours.

Pilot berth A berth or bunk for use at sea.

Pinch To sail too close to the wind so that the sails lose driving power.

Pipe cot A spare berth on a pipe frame that hinges up when not in use.

Piston hanks A hank on the luff of a staysail.

Pitch The up and down motion of the bow and stern of a boat.

Pitchpole A capsize in a following sea where the stern is lifted over the bow.

Play To adjust a sheet continuously rather than cleating it. Movement of equipment such as the rudder in its mounting or housing.

Plot To find a boat's position by laying off bearings on a chart.

Plough anchor An anchor shaped like a ploughshare similar to a CQR anchor.

Point The ability of a boat to sail close hauled: the closer she sails the better she points. A division of 11° 15' on the compass.

Poling out Using a spar to push a foresail out when running.

Pontoon A watertight tank, usually between piles, that rises and falls with the tide often with planks on top to provide a mooring.

Pooped A boat in a situation when a following sea has broken over the stern into the cockpit.

Port hand A direction on the port or left-hand side of a boat.

Port side The left-hand side of a boat when looking towards the bow.

Position line A line drawn on a chart by the navigator.

Pound A boat pounds in heavy seas when the bows drop heavily after being lifted by a wave.

Prevailing wind The wind direction that occurs most frequently at a particular place over a certain period.

Preventer A line rigged from the end of the boom to the bow in heavy weather to prevent an accidental gybe.

Privileged vessel The stand-on vessel in a collision situation: she should maintain her course and speed.

Pull To row.

Pulpit Stainless steel frame at the bow encircling the forestay to which the guardrails are attached.

Pushpit Colloquial term for the stern pulpit.

Pyrotechnic Any type of rocket or flare used for signalling. Red pyrotechnics indicate distress.

Quarter Either side of the hull between amidships and astern.

Quarter berth A berth that extends under the side deck between the cockpit and the hull.

Race A strong tidal stream.

Radar reflector A device hoisted or fitted up the mast to enhance the reflection of radar energy.

Radio direction finder (RDF) A radio receiver with a directional aerial that enables the navigator to find the direction from which a radio signal arrives.

Raft of boats Two or more boats tied up alongside each other.

Range of tide The difference between sea level at high water and sea level at the preceding or following low water.

Rate The speed of a tidal stream or current given in knots and tenths of a knot.

RDF see Radio Direction Finder.

Reach A boat is on a reach when she is neither close-hauled or running. It is her fastest point of sail.

Ready about The helmsman's shout that he intends to go about shortly.

Reciprocal course The course (or bearing) that differs from another course by 180°.

Reed A weak high-pitched fog signal.

Reef To reduce the area of sail, particularly the mainsail.

Reef points Short light lines sewn into the sail parallel with the boom that are tied under the foot (or the boom itself) when the sail is reefed.

Reefing pennants A strong line with which the luff and leech are pulled down to the boom when a sail is reefed.

Relative bearing The direction of an object relative to the fore-and-aft line of a boat measured in degrees from right ahead.

Relative wind See *Apparent wind.*

Restricted visibility Visibility restricted by rain, drizzle, fog, etc., during which vessels are required to proceed at a safe speed and to navigate with extreme caution.

Rhumb line A line on the surface of the earth that cuts all meridians at the same angle. On a standard (Mercator) chart the rhumb line appears as a straight line.

Ride To lie at anchor free to swing to the wind and tidal stream.

Ridge On a synoptic chart, a narrow area of relatively high pressure between two low pressure areas.

Riding light Alternative term for anchor light.

Riding turn On a winch the situation where an earlier turn rides over a later turn and jams.

Rigging All ropes, lines, wires and gear used to support the masts and to control the spars and sails.

Right of way Term used for the vessel which does not give way.

Risk of collision A possibility that a collision may occur; usually established by taking a compass bearing of an approaching vessel.

Roads An anchorage where the holding ground is known to be good and there is some protection from the wind and sea.

Roll The periodic rotating movement of a boat that leans alternately to port and starboard.

Roller reef A method of reefing where the sail area is reduced by rolling part of the sail around the boom.

Rolling hitch A knot used to attach a small line to a larger line or spar.

Rotator A metal spinner with vanes which rotates when a boat moves through the water actuating the log on board to which it is attached by a log line.

Round To sail around a mark.

Round turn A complete turn of a rope or line around an object. The rope completely encircles the object.

Round up To head up into the wind.

Roving fender A spare fender held ready by a crew member for use in case of emergencies.

Rowlock A U-shaped fitting which supplies a fulcrum for the oar.

Rubbing strake A projecting strake round the top of a hull to protect the hull when lying alongside.

Rudder A control surface in the water at or near the stern, used for altering course.

Run The point of sailing where a boat sails in the same direction as the wind is blowing with her sheets eased right out.

Run down To collide with another boat.

Runner A backstay that supports the mast from aft and can be slacked off.

Running fix A navigational fix when only a single landmark is available. Two bearings are taken and plotted at different times making allowance for distance travelled.

Running rigging All rigging that moves and is not part of the standing rigging.

Sacrificial anode A zinc plate fastened to the hull to prevent corrosion of metal fittings on the hull.

Sail locker Place where sails are stowed.

Sail ties Light lines used to lash a lowered sail to the boom or guardrails to prevent it blowing about.

Sailing directions Also called Pilots. Official publications covering specific areas containing navigational information concerning, for example, coasts, harbours and tides.

Sailing free Not close hauled; sailing with sheets eased out.

Saloon The main cabin.

Salvage The act of saving a vessel from danger at sea.

Samson post Strong fitting bolted firmly to the deck around which anchor cables, mooring lines or tow ropes are made fast.

SAR Search and Rescue.

Scend Vertical movement of waves or swell against, for example, a harbour wall.

Scope The ratio of the length of anchor cable let out to the depth of water.

Scupper Drain hole in the toe-rail.

Sea anchor A device, such as a conical canvas bag open at both ends, streamed from bow or stern to hold a boat bow or stern on to the wind or sea.

Sea breeze A daytime wind blowing across a coastline from the sea caused by the rising air from the heating of the land by the sun.

Sea legs The ability to keep one's feet in spite of the motion of the boat.

Seacock A stopcock next to every inlet and outlet in the hull to prevent accidental entry of water.

Searoom An area in which a vessel can navigate without difficulty or danger of hitting an obstruction.

Seaway A stretch of water where there are waves.

Securite An internationally recognised safety signal used on the radio telephone preceding an important navigational or meteorological warning.

Seize To bind two ropes together.

Serve To cover and protect a splice on a rope by binding with small line or twine.

Set (sails) To hoist a sail.

Set (Tidal stream) The direction in which a tidal stream or current flows.

Set sail To start out on a voyage.

Shackle A metal link for connecting ropes, wires or chains to sails, anchors, etc. To shackle on is to connect using a shackle.

Shape A ball, cone or diamond shaped object, normally black, hoisted by day on a vessel to indicate a special state or occupation.

Sheave A wheel over which a rope or wire runs.

Sheer off To turn away from another vessel or object in the water.

Sheet Rope or line fastened to the clew of a sail or the end of the boom supporting it. Named after the sail to which it is attached.

Sheet bend A knot used to join two ropes of different size together.

Sheet in To pull in on a sheet till it is taut and the sail drawing.

Shelving A gradual slope in the seabed.

Shipping forecast Weather forecast broadcast four times each day by the British Broadcasting Corporation for the benefit of those at sea.

Shipping lane A busy track across the sea or ocean.

Shipshape Neat and efficient.

Shoal An area offshore where the water is so shallow that a ship might run aground. To shoal is to become shallow.

Shock cord Elastic rubber bands enclosed in a sheath of fibres, very useful for lashing.

Shorten in Decrease the amount of anchor cable let out.

Shorten sail To reduce the amount of sail set either by reefing or changing to a smaller sail.

Shrouds Parts of the standing rigging that support the mast laterally.

Sidedeck The deck alongside the coachroof.

Sidelight The red and green lights exhibited either side of the bows by vessels under way and making way through the water.

Sill A wall which acts as a dam, to keep water in a marina.

Siren The fog signal made by vessels over 12 metres in length when under way.

Skeg A false keel fitted near the stern which supports the leading edge of the rudder.

Skylight A framework fitted on the deck of a boat with glazed windows to illuminate the cabin and provide ventilation.

Slab reef A method of reefing a boomed sail where the sail is flaked down on top of the boom.

Slack off To ease or pay out a line.

Slack water In tidal waters, the period of time when the tidal stream is non-existent or negligible.

Slam When the underpart of the forward part of the hull hits the water when pitching in heavy seas.

Slide A metal or plastic fitting on the luff or foot of a sail running in a track on the mast or boom.

Sliding hatch A sliding hatch fitted over the entrance to the cabin.

Slip To let go quickly.

Slip lines Mooring ropes or lines doubled back so that they can be let go easily from on board.

Slipway An inclined ramp leading into the sea.

Snap hook A hook that springs shut when released.

Snap shackle A shackle that is held closed by a spring-loaded plunger.

Snarl up Lines or ropes that are twisted or entangled.

Snatch Jerk caused by too short an anchor cable in a seaway. To take a turn quickly around a cleat, bollard or samson post.

Snug down To prepare for heavy weather by securing all loose gear.

Soldier's wind A wind that enables a sailing boat to sail to her destination and return without beating.

Sole The floor of a cabin or cockpit.

SOS International distress signal made by light, sound or radio.

Sound To measure the depth of water.

Sounding The depth of water below chart datum.

Sou'wester A waterproof oilskin hat with a broad rim.

Spar General term for all poles used on board such as mast, boom and yard.

Speed made good The speed made good over the ground; that is, the boat speed corrected for tidal stream and leeway.

Spill wind To ease the sheets so that the sail is only partly filled by the wind, the rest being spilt.

Spindrift Fine spray blown off wave crests by strong winds.

Spinnaker A large symmetrical balloon shaped sail used when running or reaching.

Spinnaker pole A spar which is used to hold the spinnaker out.

Spit A projecting shoal or strip of land connected to the shore.

Splice A permanent join made between two ropes.

Split ring A ring like a key ring that can be fed into an eye to prevent accidental withdrawal.

Spray hood A folding canvas cover over the entrance to the cabin.

Spreaders Metal struts fitted either side of the mast to spread the shrouds out sideways.

Spring tide The tides at which the range is greatest: the height of high water is greater and that for low water is less than those for neap tides.

Springs Mooring lines fastened to prevent a boat moving forwards or backwards relative to the quay or other boats alongside.

Squall A sudden increase of wind speed often associated with a line of low dark clouds representing an advancing cold front.

Stanchions Metal posts supporting the guardrails.

Standby to gybe A warning given by the helmsman that he is about to gybe.

Stand in To head towards land.

Stand off To head away from the shore.

Stand-on vessel The boat that does not have to keep clear; it must maintain course and speed.

Standing rigging Wire rope or solid rods that support masts and fixed spars but do not control the sails.

Starboard side The right-hand side when looking forward towards the bow.

Stay Part of the standing rigging which provides support fore and aft.

Staysail A sail set on a stay.

Steady Order to the helmsman to keep the boat on her present course.

Steaming light Alternative term for masthead light.

Steep-to A sharply sloping seabed.

Steerage way A boat has steerage way when she is moving fast enough to answer to the helm; that is, to respond to deflections of the rudder.

Steering compass The compass permanently mounted adjacent to the helmsman which he uses as a reference to keep the boat on a given course.

Stem The forewardmost part of the hull.

Stemhead The top of the stem.

Stemhead fitting A fitting on the stemhead, often an anchor roller.

Stern The afterpart of the boat.

Stern gland Packing around the propeller shaft where it passes through the hull.

Stern light A white light exhibited from the stern.

Stern line The mooring line going aft from the stern.

Sternsheets The aftermost part of an open boat.

Stiff A boat that does not heel easily; opposite to tender.

Stopper knot A knot made in the end of a rope to prevent it running out through a block or fairlead.

Storm Wind of Beaufort force 10, 48 to 55 knots; or a violent storm force 11, 56 to 63 knots.

Storm jib Small heavy jib set in strong winds.

Stormbound Confined to a port or anchorage by heavy weather.

Stove in A hull that has been broken inwards.

Stow Put away in a proper place. Stowed for sea implies that all gear and loose equipment has, in addition, been lashed down.

Strand To run a vessel aground intentionally or accidentally.

Strop A loop of wire rope fitted round a spar. A wire rope used to add length to the luff of a headsail.

Strum box A strainer fitted around the suction end of a bilge pump hose to prevent the pump being choked by debris.

Strut A small projecting rod.

Suit A complete set of sails.

Surge To ease a rope out round a winch or bollard.

Swashway A narrow channel between shoals.

Sweat up To tauten a rope as much as possible.

Sweep A long oar.

Swig To haul a line tight when it is under load by pulling it out at right angles and quickly taking in the slack.

Swing To rotate sideways on a mooring in response to a change in direction of the tidal stream or wind.

Swinging room The area encompassed by a swing that excludes any risk of collision or of grounding.

Synopsis A brief statement outlining the weather situation at a particular time.

Synoptic chart A weather chart covering a large area on which is plotted information giving an overall view of the weather at a particular moment.

Tack To go about from one course to another with the bow passing through the eye of the wind. A sailing boat is on a tack if she is neither gybing nor tacking.

Tack The lower forward corner of a sail.

Tackle A combination of rope and blocks designed to increase the pulling or hoisting power of a line.

Take in Lower a sail.

Take the helm Steer the boat.

Take way off To reduce the speed of the boat.

Telltales Lengths of wool or ribbon attached to the sails or shrouds to indicate the airflow or apparent direction of the wind.

Tender A boat that heels easily is said to be tender; the opposite of stiff. Also small dinghy used to take crew to a larger boat.

Thwart The athwartships seat in a small boat or dinghy.

Tidal stream The horizontal movement of water caused by the tides.

Tidal stream atlas An official publication showing the direction and rate of the tidal streams for a particular area.

Tide The vertical rise and fall of the water in the oceans in response to the gravitational forces of the sun and moon.

Tide tables Official annual publication which gives the times and heights of high and low water for standard ports and the differences for secondary ports.

Tideway The part of a channel where the tidal stream runs most strongly.

Tiller A lever attached to the rudder head by which the helmsman deflects the rudder.

Time (4-figure notation) Time is given in a 4-figure notation based on the 24-hour clock.

Toe-rail A low strip of wood or light alloy that runs round the edge of a deck.

Toggle A small piece of wood inserted in an eye to make a quick connection.

Topping lift A line from the base of the mast passing around a sheave at the top then to the end of the boom to take the weight of the boom when lowering the sail.

Topsides The part of a boat which lies above the waterline when she is not heeled.

Track The path between two positions: ground track is that over the ground; water track is that through the water.

Traffic separation scheme In areas of heavy traffic, a system of one-way lanes. Special regulations apply to shipping in these zones.

Transceiver A radio transmitter and receiver.

Transducer A component that converts electric signals into sound waves and vice versa.

Transferred position line A position line for one time, transferred, with due allowance for the vessel's ground track, to cross with another position line at a later time.

Transit Two fixed objects are in transit when they are in line.

Transom The flat transverse structure across the stern of a hull.

Traveller The sliding car on a track, for example on the mainsheet track or adjustable headsail sheet block.

Trick Spell on duty, especially at the helm.

Tri-colour light A single light at the top of the mast of sailing boats under 20 metres long that can be used when sailing in place of the navigation lights.

Trim To adjust the sails by easing or hardening in the sheets to obtain maximum driving force.

Trip-line A line attached to the crown of an anchor to enable it to be pulled out backwards if it gets caught fast by an object on the sea-bed.

Trot Mooring buoys laid in a line.

Truck The very top of the mast.

Trysail A small heavy sail set on the mast in stormy weather in place of the mainsail.

Tune To improve the performance of a sailing boat or engine.

Twilight Period before sunrise and after sunset when it is not quite dark.

Twine Small line used for sewing and whipping.

Unbend To unshackle sheets and halyards and remove a sail ready to stow.

Underway A vessel is underway if it is not at anchor, made fast to the shore or aground.

Unshackle To unfasten.

Unship To remove an object from its working position.

Up and down Said of an anchor cable when it is vertical.

Uphaul A line which is used to raise a spar vertically.

Upstream The direction from which a river flows.

Upwind The direction from which the wind is blowing.

Vang A tackle or strap fitted between the boom and the toe-rail to keep the boom horizontal.

Variation The angle between the true and the magnetic meridian for any geographical position.

Veer Of a cable or line, to pay out gradually. Of the wind, to change direction clockwise.

Ventilator (vent) A fitting which allows fresh air to enter the boat.

VHF Very High Frequency; usually taken as meaning the VHF radio telephone.

Visibility The greatest distance at which an object can be seen against its background.

Wake Disturbed water left by a moving boat. The direction of the wake compared with the fore-and-aft line of the boat is often used as a rough measure of leeway.

Warp Heavy lines used for mooring, kedging or towing, and to move a boat by hauling on warps secured to a bollard or buoy.

Wash The turbulent water left astern by a moving boat.

Washboards Removable planks fitted in the cabin entrance to prevent water getting in.

Watch One of the periods into which 24 hours is divided on board.

Waterline The line along the hull at the surface of the water in which she floats.

Wear To change tacks by gybing.

Weather a mark To succeed in passing to windward of a mark.

Weather helm The tendency of a boat to turn her bow to windward making it necessary to hold the tiller to the weather side.

Weep To leak slowly.

Weigh anchor To raise the anchor.

Well A sump in the bilges. A small locker for the anchor.

Wheel The steering wheel that moves the rudder.

Whipping Twine bound round the ends of a rope to keep it from fraying.

Whisker pole Light spar to hold out the clew of a headsail when running, particularly when goosewinged.

Whistle An appliance to make sound signals in restricted visibility and when manoeuvring.

White horses Breaking waves with foamy crest. Not surf breaking on the shore.

Winch A fitting designed to assist the crew hauling on a rope or line.

Winch handle A removable handle used for operating a winch.

Windage All parts of a boat that contribute to total air drag.

Windlass The winch used for weighing the anchor.

Windward The direction from which the wind blows.

Withies Branches used in small rivers to mark the edges of the channel.

Yankee jib A large jib set forward of the staysail in light winds.

Yard A long spar on which a square sail is set.

Yawing Swinging from side to side of the course set, or at anchor.

Yawl A two-masted boat where the mizzen mast is aft of the rudder stock.

Index